PAPAL AND EPISCOPAL ADMINISTRATION OF CHURCH PROPERTY

THE CATHOLIC UNIVERSITY OF AMERICA
CANON LAW STUDIES
No. 147

PAPAL AND EPISCOPAL ADMINISTRATION OF CHURCH PROPERTY

AN HISTORICAL SYNOPSIS AND COMMENTARY

BY THE

REV. JOSEPH J. COMYNS, C.SS.R., A.B., J.C.L.
Priest of the Baltimore Province

A DISSERTATION

Submitted to the Faculty of Canon Law of the Catholic University of America in Partial Fulfillment of the Requirements for the Degree of Doctor of Canon Law

THE CATHOLIC UNIVERSITY OF AMERICA PRESS
WASHINGTON, D. C.
1942

Imprimi Potest:

GULIELMUS T. MCCARTY, C.SS.R.,
Superior Provincialis.
Brooklynii, N. Y., die XXV Aprilis, 1942.

Nihil Obstat:

ARTURUS J. SCANLAN, S.T.D.,
Censor Librorum.
Neo Eboraci, N. Y., die VI Maii, 1942.

Imprimatur:

✠ FRANCISCUS J. SPELLMAN, D.D.,
Archiepiscopus Neo-Eboracensis.
Neo Eboraci, N. Y., die VI Maii, 1942.

Printed by
THE PAULIST PRESS
New York, N. Y.
51

TO

JESUS CHRIST

OUR KING AND LAWGIVER

AND TO

OUR MOTHER OF PERPETUAL HELP

TABLE OF CONTENTS

PAGE

LIST OF ABBREVIATIONS

AAS—*Acta Apostolicae Sedis.*
AER—*American Ecclesiastical Review.*
AKKR—*Archiv für katholisches Kirchenrecht.*
Fontes—*Codicis Iuris Canonici Fontes.*
C.—*Codex* (Justinianus).
Coll. Lac.—*Collectio Lacensis.*
MPG—Migne, J. P., *Patrologiae Cursus Completus—Series Graeca.*
MPL—Migne, J. P., *Patrologiae Cursus Completus—Series Latina.*
Nov.—*Novella.*
Pont. Comm. Intr.—*Pontificia Commissio ad Codicis Canones Authentice Interpretandos.*

FOREWORD

Although the primary purpose of the Church is the salvation of souls, it is clear that material means are necessary if the Church is to perform its primary duty efficiently and thoroughly. The great importance which temporal goods have in the plan of the Church is seen from the detailed legislation which has marked the efforts of the lawmakers throughout the entire history of the Christian era properly to safeguard ecclesiastical patrimonies. Moreover, penalties for the violations of these laws have been severe.

The purpose of this work is to investigate the rights and duties of the principal administrators of ecclesiastical property, namely the pope and the bishops.

The first part of the work traces their activities, rights and duties before the promulgation of the present Code of Canon Law. The second part of the dissertation concerns itself with the present legislation in the same sphere.

No attempt has been made to study the law of the Church with regard to the acquisition and alienation of ecclesiastical property. These topics have received detailed treatment in other works in the *Canon Law Studies* of the School of Canon Law at the Catholic University of America. Due to the fact that even a summary of the Civil Law is manifestly impossible in a treatise of this kind, only incidental references are made to the prevailing civil law, and then only when the ecclesiastical law makes explicit reference to it.

Although the present status of ecclesiastical law with regard to church property represents a vast improvement over the past, nevertheless there are many difficulties which have not received a definite solution from the legislator. It is hoped that in the treatment of these difficulties the opinions of the eminent commentators have been clearly presented and respectfully weighed in anticipation of specific conclusions.

The writer takes this occasion to express his thankful appreciation to his present provincial superior, the Very Rev. William T. McCarty, C.SS.R., for the opportunity to continue the advanced course of studies which his predecessor, the Very Rev. Andrew Kuhn, C.SS.R., had so graciously offered to the author. It is also a pleasure to take advantage of this occasion to express appreciation for the help afforded the author by the Faculty of the School of Canon Law, as well as for the aid so kindly offered to him by his confreres, relatives and friends.

CHAPTER I

INTRODUCTORY NOTIONS

Administration, as applied to ecclesiastical property, is defined as: The control or care of the temporal goods of the Church in order that they may serve the purposes for which they were acquired. This definition includes all acts which are necessary or useful: (1) To keep the property in good condition; (2) To make it productive; (3) To derive benefit from it; (4) To apply, pay out and use it for legitimate purposes.[1]

Although canon 1527 deals with the effects of unauthorized acts of *extraordinary* administration and presupposes a distinction between these and the acts of ordinary administration, the legislator neither here nor in any canon of the Code gives a list of such acts. As Pistocchi well says,[2] it is rather difficult to indicate a norm which will distinguish clearly the two general classes of acts. The norm would have to include the regulations not only of the general laws of the Church, but also of the particular laws of plenary and provincial councils and of diocesan synods and enactments, as well as the particular precepts of local ordinaries which do not contradict rights granted by a higher superior. For, what the common law does not forbid one to do without the previous permission of a superior, the particular law may prohibit under pain of invalidity.[3] Thus, for example, although by common law the pastor has the right to use the money of the parish for its benefit in other than current expenses, since he is not forbidden to do so unless the expense involves

[1] Wernz, *Ius Decretalium* (2. ed., Romae: Typographia Polyglotta, 1908), III, n. 147; Vermeersch-Creusen, *Epitome Iuris Canonici* (3. ed., Mechliniae et Romae: Dessain, 1927-1928), II, 520; McManus, *The Administration of Temporal Goods in Religious Institutes,* The Catholic University of America, Canon Law Studies, n. 109 (Washington: The Catholic University of America, 1937), p. 12.

[2] *De Bonis Ecclesiae Temporalibus* (Taurini: Marietti, 1932), p. 367.

[3] Larraona, "Commentarium Codicis,"—*CpR,* XII (1931), 356; McManus, *The Administration of Temporal Goods in Religious Institutes,* p. 81.

the contracting of an unauthorized debt or the execution of a forbidden alienation of ecclesiastical goods, yet by particular law he may spend only a certain percentage of the annual income of the parish. If he spends more than this allowance he exceeds the limits of ordinary administration.[4]

Therefore, since it is manifestly impossible to determine in detail all of the acts of ordinary administration, this introductory chapter will attempt merely to state the general norms which distinguish administrative acts, and then will indicate what acts the Code considers as part of *extraordinary* administration, that is, acts which exceed the *"ex officio"* power of the administrator.

The general rules which serve to show the distinction between acts of ordinary and extraordinary administration may be indicated thus: acts of ordinary administration are those which the administrator may perform validly by reason of his office and without the permission of the superior. Such acts are regularly and frequently necessary for the upkeep of the property and for meeting current expenses. However, if some of these acts which are necessary as part of the administrative office are of greater importance, then the law may require that the administrator obtain the superior's permission, at least for the lawfulness of the acts. Under such a requirement the acts do not exceed the administrative power of the pastor or other administrator. They are valid even if performed without the necessary permission. However, if the law requires that certain administrative acts must have the permission of the competent superior

[4] *Acta et Decreta Concilii Provincialis Portlandensis in Oregon Quarti* (1932), Appendix, nn. 3, 5.

N. 3. "No pastor or administrator may spend from the parish funds, in one calendar year, for other than current expenses, an amount exceeding $500.00, without the expressed permission in writing of the Bishop, provided the total parish income exceeds $5,000.00; if such income is more than $2,500.00 and less than $5,000.00, the sum of $250.00; if such income is less than $2,500.00, the sum of $100.00 for other than current expenses.

N. 5. "As no pastor, administrator, priest or committee or any member thereof is the agent of the Bishop, or the agent of the parish beyond the limits of articles one, two and three, no contracts, liability or obligation beyond these limits without the special written authorization of the Bishop shall be in the absence of such special written authorization or ratification of the Bishop other than the personal contract, indebtedness or liability of such person. . . . "

in order that they may be juridically valid, then the administrator who performs such acts without permission acts invalidly. These are acts of extraordinary administration.[5] If the law says that an act is invalid without the required permission, or if the law requires a special faculty in the administrator before his act will be valid, then those acts which are so conditioned are to be considered acts of extraordinary administration.[6]

Among the acts of ordinary administration which under the general law require no special permission even for the lawfulness of the acts are: the receipt of income of any kind, such as rent, church collections, interest, etc.; the expenses necessary for the operation of the church and parochial buildings; the deposit of superfluous money in banks for security, and in general any acts which are regularly necessary for the management of the property of the moral person. Acts of ordinary administration which either because of their infrequency or in view of their importance may not be classed as regularly necessary have been mentioned above, namely, participation in lawsuits, the refusal of the donations which have been made to the Church, and the investment of money which does not belong

[5] Vromant, *De Bonis Ecclesiae Temporalibus,* pp. 195-196; Larraona, "Commentarium Codicis,"—*CpR,* XII (1931), 356; DeMeester, *Compendium Iuris Canonici et Iuris Canonico-Civilis* (3 vols. in 4, Brugis, 1921-1928), tomus III, pars I, 399; Blat, *Commentarium Textus Codicis Iuris Canonici* (6 vols. Romae, 1921-1927), lib. III, pars II-VI, 540; McManus, *The Administration of Temporal Goods in Religious Institutes,* pp. 80-82.

[6] McManus, *The Administration of Temporal Goods in Religious Institutes,* p. 82. The use of the word *"facultas"* generally signifies validity, while *"licentia"* refers to lawfulness of action, unless there is an express or equivalent invalidating clause attached. For example, canons 1044-1045 and 1050 use the former and imply it as a condition for validity. Canons 1527, § 1, 1530, § 1, 3° and 1532, § 4, use *"licentia"* and add an invalidating clause; canons 1526 and 1536, § 2, mention *"licentia"* without any invalidating clause, and then the permission is required only for the lawfulness of the act. Although a faculty in the broad sense of the term may be practically the same as *"licentia,"* nevertheless in the strict meaning of the word it signifies a grant of power which is necessary for the inferior to act validly. Cf. Putzer, *Commentarium in Facultates Apostolicas* (4. ed., New York: Benziger, 1897), p. 2; Cocchi, *Commentarium,* I, 183; Motry, *Diocesan Faculties According to the Code of Canon Law,* The Catholic University of America, Canon Law Studies, n. 16 (Washington, D. C.: Catholic University of America, 1922), pp. 15, 20.

to any capital sum, that is, to any sum set aside for the purchase of immovable property, or to support the moral person with its revenue.[7]

Acts of extraordinary administration, that is, those which require the previous permission of the competetent superior for the validity of the acts, are acts designated as such in the law, and especially in the general law acts of alienation both in the strict and in the broad sense of the word. The strict sense signifies a donation, exchange or sale of immovable property. The broad sense of the term signifies any contract which renders the temporal condition of the Church less secure.[8]

Among the acts of the latter class are the issuance of mortgages, the giving of property as security, the contracting of debts, even for just causes; [9] the lease of church property for more than nine years,[10] the acceptance in one payment of the full amount of the rental for the use and usufruct of land which originally had been let out with the agreement that it would bring in a stipulated rental at stated intervals. However, it must be noted that in order to protect the property of the Church, the law requires that the competent superior shall not give consent in this case, unless the amount of the full rental which is accepted is sufficient to enable the ecclesiastical administrator so to invest it that it will bring in the same income.[11] Among other acts which render church property less secure and are therefore acts of extraordinary administration are the remission of debts to the debtor, the cession of the right to judicial action which

[7] Canons 1526; 1536, § 2; 1523, 4°.

[8] Canons 1530-1533. Vromant, *De Bonis Ecclesiae Temporalibus* (Lovanii: Museum Lessianum, 1934), p. 235. "Alienation is any act or contract whereby church property is exposed to danger of loss, or its legal possession is reduced to a worse condition. It is that act by which property, real rights, or possessions of any ecclesiastical moral person are gratuitously or onerously transferred, set aside, lessened, or burdened."—Cleary, *Canonical Limitations on the Alienation of Church Property,* The Catholic University of America, Canon Law Studies, n. 100 (Washington: The Catholic University of America, 1936), p. 2. Cf. Wernz, *Ius Decretalium,* III, n. 154.

[9] Canon 1538, § 1.

[10] Canon 1541.

[11] Canon 1542, § 1. Cf. Ayrinhac, *Administrative Legislation in the New Code of Canon Law* (London, New York, Toronto: Longmans, Green, 1930), pp. 455-456.

alone will protect church property, the relinquishment of an active servitude or the toleration of a passive servitude,[12] and other acts which may be specified in the particular legislation of the various dioceses.

Vromant [13] claims that the erection of a church is an act of extraordinary administration. He appeals to canon 1162 in support of his contention. However, apart from the fact that this canon does not apply to the economic or financial factor involved, but rather to the hierarchical order which must be observed, it should also be noted that the canon makes no mention of invalidity, either expressly or equivalently, and therefore it must be presumed to be an act of ordinary administration which is indeed of such grave importance that it requires a previous permission from the competent superior.[14]

The present general law of the Church with regard to acts of extraordinary administration is very much like the laws enacted for the dioceses of Holland in 1856.[15] The two laws are not identical, for the particular law considered as acts of extraordinary administration such acts as are now considered acts of more important ordinary administration, namely, the erection of a church and the initiation of litigation in court as a representative of the church.[16] The reason for this difference is that the general law of the Church does not require a special permission or faculty under pain of invalidity for the performance of such acts.

Before an attempt is made to view the age-old practice of the

[12] Wernz, *Ius Decretalium,* III, n. 154; Vromant, *De Bonis Ecclesiae Temporalibus,* p. 235. An active servitude is the right to *use* another's property, for example, a road or a waterway; a passive servitude is the admission of the same right over one's own property to another. Cf. Leage, *Roman Private Law* (2. ed. Ziegler, London: Macmillan, 1930), pp. 177-178.

[13] *Op. cit.*, pp. 198, 235.

[14] Canon 1162, § 1. "Nulla ecclesia aedificetur sine expresso Ordinarii loci consensu scriptis dato, quem tamen Vicarius Generalis praestare nequit sine mandato speciali."

[15] S. C. de Prop. Fide (C. G.), 21 iul. 1856, art. 20, *Coll. S. C. P. F.*, I, n. 1127; *Fontes,* n. 4841.

[16] Cf. canons 1162, § 1 and 1526.

Church in the management of its own property, it is proper to demonstrate the right of the Church to administer its possessions, a right which has been questioned by certain rulers and attacked by divers philosophers.[17] This right flows necessarily from the right to acquire and possess property, since the dominion of a thing carries with it the power to use that thing as one sees fit, unless the exercise of this right endangers the common good or the inalienable rights of other individuals.[18] Since the Church is a perfect society, that is, one which is in its own order self-sufficient and independent,[19] and since in its aim it is superior to all other societies of men,[20] it has a right to possess and consequently a right to administer all the means necessary to attain its end. As a visible society the Church requires material means to carry on its work of preaching the gospel to the entire world. Hence, as the Angelic Doctor declares, natural reason demands that the Church have the power to possess and administer its own property.[21]

Since the very basis of property administration is the proprietorship of the goods to be administered, it is necessary to make clear who actually has the dominion of any particular parcel of property. The Code clearly states that each moral person in the Church has the right to own the goods which it acquires by a legitimate title, and that this right of proprietorship is under the supreme power of the Holy See.[22] Since the right to administer property goes hand in hand with the dominion over property, the right to care for and administer property may belong to any moral person in the Church, unless some particular moral person has been forbidden to acquire property. However, since moral persons, as such, cannot administer their holdings, this right and duty belongs to him who has been

[17] Cf. Pius X, litt. encycl. *Une fois encore,* 6 ian. 1907—*Fontes,* n. 677.

[18] Marc-Gestermann, *Institutiones Morales* (17. ed., Lyons: 1922), I, 547.

[19] Cf. Cavagnis, *Institutiones Iuris Publici Ecclesiastici* (2. ed., Romae, 1888), I, 29.

[20] Cf. Ottaviani, *Institutiones Iuris Publici Ecclesiastici* (2. ed., Romae, 1935), I, 186.

[21] St. Thomas Aquinas, *Summa Theologica* (14. ed., Parisiis, 1885, IIa, IIae, q. 87, art. 1, in corp.

[22] Canons 1495, § 2, and 1499, § 2.

designated lawfully as the administrator of the property of the moral person.[23]

Because the administrator is not the owner of the property, he may not distribute it or dispose of it arbitrarily. Rather, he must follow the norms which govern his office and which have been established by competent superiors. He has the duty to protect the property which he administers and, if possible, to improve it.[24]

This dissertation treats of ecclesiastical property. The Code uses the phrase "*bona temporalia*" to signify this idea.[25] According to canon 1497, § 1, property may be *corporeal* or *incorporeal*. *Corporeal* property signifies those possessions which can be felt or touched, such as houses, cattle, land, furniture, etc. *Incorporeal* property is that which has no tangible existence, but which exists legally. This includes the right to property, the right to use another's property, the right to collect debts, etc. These cannot be felt or touched, but they have a money value. In such a case they come under the classification of property.[26] Corporeal property may be either *movable* or *immovable*. The reason for this division inheres in the basic distinction which exists between land and the things attached to the land (immovable property) and all other property which in its nature is not stationary (movable property). Movable things sometimes are by reason of a legal enactment considered as immovable property. Thus, for example, a sum of money which has been especially destined for the purchase of immovable property, or for the construction of a church, or for the extreme needs of some church, is considered by some commentators to be immovable property, provided that the designation of the money has been made with the consent of the superior and his council.[27]

23 Wernz, *Ius Decretalium*, III, n. 157.

24 C. 2, *de religiosis domibus, ut episcopo sint subjectae*, III, 11, in Clem.; c. 2, X, *de donationibus*, III, 24.

25 Cf. canons 1495, 1497; etc.

26 Cf. Leage, *Roman Private Law*, pp. 137-138; Blat, *Commentarium Textus Codicis Iuris Canonici*, lib. III, pars II-VI, 534.

27 Vromant, *De Bonis Ecclesiae Temporalibus*, p. 51; Reiffenstuel, *Ius Canonicum Universum*, III, tit. 13, n. 15; McManus, *The Administration of Temporal Goods in Religious Institutes*, p. 2.

Corporeal and incorporeal goods alike may become ecclesiastical property. They become such when title is acquired to them by the Catholic Church Universal, by the Apostolic See, or by any inferior ecclesiastical moral person, namely, by a subordinate juridical entity which has received its capacity as a subject of rights and duties either by a special decree of competent ecclesiastical authority or by the declaration of the ecclesiastical law itself.[28]

[28] Canon 100, § 1.

Part One

Historical Development

CHAPTER II

THE ADMINISTRATION OF ECCLESIASTICAL PROPERTY IN ROMAN LAW

In the first centuries of the Christian era the Church actually acquired and administered property, such as cemeteries and churches.[1] The bishop was the administrator of charity to the sick, widows and captives.[2] However, the right of property administration was very insecure before the time of the Emperors Galerius (305-311) and Constantine (306-337). In fact, during the era of persecution the Christians had no civil rights in this matter,[3] except for rare intervals of imperial favor, for example, when Gallienus (260-268), the son of Valerian (253-260), restored to the Christians their cemeteries and churches[4] which they had erected in peaceful times, perhaps by reason of the law of Septimius Severus (193-211) concerning the *Collegia Funeraticia.*[5]

In the year 303 Diocletian ordered the destruction of the Christian churches.[6] In view of this it is unlikely that the Church had any civil property rights. Galerius, who had really inspired the

[1] Le Clercq, *Manuel D'Archéologie Chrétienne,* I, 323; Lanciani, *Pagan and Christian Rome,* p. 111. Cf. Doheny, *Church Property: Modes of Acquisition,* The Catholic University of America, Canon Law Studies, n. 41 (Washington: The Catholic University of America, 1927), p. 16.

[2] St. Justin, *Apologia,* I, n. 67—*MPG,* VI, 430.

[3] Gaston Coulondre, *Des Acquisitions de biens par les éstablissements de la religion chrétienne in droit romain et dans l'ancien droit Français* (Paris: Rousseau, 1886), p. 17.

[4] Eusebius, *Historia Ecclesiastica,* lib. VII, c. 13—*MPG,* XX, 674.

[5] De Rossi, *Roma Sotteranea,* I, 101-110. Cf. Funk, *Manual of Church History,* I, 45.

[6] Lactantius, *De Mortibus Persecutorum,* c. 12—*MPL,* VII, 214.

destructive work of his predecessor Diocletian, rather hesitantly granted a certain amount of toleration to the Church during his reign.[7] He declared that the Christians could exist as a group with moral personality. This was the first time in the history of the empire that the Christian religion was recognized as a *religio licita.* It may be surmised that, by granting the Christians the right to establish their churches and meeting places, Galerius showed his will to recognize as legal the property rights of the Church, although he made no manifestation of intention to restore its confiscated property.[8] Constantine went further and restored this confiscated property to the Church.[9]

In 321 Constantine enacted a law permitting the Church to receive property bequeathed by last will and testament.[10] This permission continued in force throughout the following century,[11] although in the year 390 there seemed to be some need to restrain the avarice of certain clerics who attempted to deprive legitimate heirs of their rightful inheritance.[12]

Late in the fifth century Marcianus (450-457) decreed that widows, deaconesses and religious women could leave their possessions to the Church.[13] In the sixth century, when the Emperor Justinian decided that Roman Law needed codification, Constantine's declaration concerning testamentary donations in favor of the Church was renewed.[14] In 528 Justinian decreed that the Church could receive and administer donations for pious causes, but he made the restriction that gifts which exceeded five hundred *solidos* had to be conveyed by a written instrument, unless the emperor made the gift.[15]

[7] Lactantius, *op. cit.,* c. 34—*MPL,* VII, 249.

[8] Knipfing, "Religious Toleration during the Reign of Constantine," *American Catholic Historical Review,* N. S., IV (1924-1925), 492 ff.

[9] Lactantius, *De Mortibus Persecutorum,* c. 48—*MPL,* VII, 267 ff. Cf. Kirch, *Enchiridion Fontium Historiae Ecclesiasticorum Antiquae* (4. ed., Friburgi Brisgoviae: Herder, 1923), n. 353.

[10] *Codex Theodosianus,* XVI, 2, 4.

[11] C. Th., XVI, 2, 38.

[12] Cf. C. Th., XVI, 2, 28.

[13] *Leges Novellae ad Theodosianum Pertinentes* (455), Nov. V.

[14] C. (1, 2) 1.

[15] C. (1, 2) 19, 23.

Although the Roman Law took some notice of the pope as the supreme head of the Church,[16] nevertheless it seems that no specific recognition was accorded to him as the supreme administrator of the temporal goods of the Church. The law in general dealt with the rights and duties of the bishop, econome and inferior administrators.

Article 1. The Bishop as Administrator

It seems that the sources acknowledge that the bishop had the supervision of all ecclesiastical property in his diocese and in certain conditions even a direct and immediate administrative power over it.

His supervisory power included the right to determine the amount of money to be spent for the construction of churches and for the support of the ministers; [17] to take action against those who had failed to fulfill promises of donations to pious causes; [18] to substitute new executors of pious wills if the ones whom the testator named did not fulfill the specific obligations of the testator; [19] to examine the financial administration of the economes and other inferior administrators who were subject to him; [20] to act as judge in lawsuits which involved ecclesiastical property; [21] and to give previous consent to those who planned to erect monasteries, or who planned to pay church debts, by granting long-term leases of immovable property.[22]

In addition to his supervisory power the bishop had the right under certain conditions directly to administer also such property which did not belong to the diocese as such. Thus, if a certain sum had been left for the redemption of captives and no person had been designated to execute the bequest, the bishop had the right to see to it that the will of the testator was fulfilled.[23] He had the right to divide pious bequests for the poor, when the latter had not been

[16] Nov. CXXXI, 2.
[17] Nov. LXVII, 2.
[18] C. (1, 2) 15.
[19] Nov. CXXXI, 10.
[20] C. (1, 3) 41, 10; Nov. CXXIII, 23.
[21] C. (1, 4) 13; Nov. CXXIII, 21.
[22] Nov. V, 1; CXXXI, 7; CXX, 6, 1.
[23] C. (1, 3) 28, 1.

specified and on the condition that neither he nor his econome nor the church had a share in the division.[24] Moreover, it seems that there were many churches whose expenses were paid by the bishop.[25]

Despite the fact that the sources seem to indicate that churches apart from the episcopal church had their own administration,[26] it is not clear that in the ordinary factors of their administration parochial churches were independent of the episcopal church. For it may well have been that the churches which had their own administration, at least with regard to expenses, derived this right from the money that was left in a pious will by the founder,[27] or that the church was a monastic church without parochial status.[28]

Aside from the possibilities contemplated immediately above concerning the origin of a separate administration, there are evidences that even in the early times of parochial units the bishop retained the immediate administrative power with regard to parochial property.[29] Therefore, since the sources seem to make no specific mention of a separate administration for the property of parish churches, the conclusion seems to follow that the bishop was the immediate administrator of such church property which belonged to the other churches or parishes of the diocese. If other clerics had a share in the administration, it seems that they enjoyed it by a delegated rather than by any ordinary power attached to their office.[30]

[24] C. (1, 3) 48, 3; Nov. CXXXI, 11.

[25] "In ceteris autem ecclesiis omnibus, quarum sumptus sanctissima magna ecclesia facit, . . ." Nov. III, 2.

[26] "Et si quidem sanctissimae ecclesiae sint vel aliae venerabiles domus, quarum administrationem sanctissimus eius loci episcopus vel per se vel per venerabilem eius clerum exercet, . . . Quodsi ptochia vel xenones vel nosocomia vel aliae venerabiles domus sint propriam administrationem habentes, si quidem forte sanctae domus oratoriae sint, voluntate maioris partis clericorum qui ibi ministeria obeunt, . . ." Nov. CXX, 6, 1. "Sed ne in reliquis quidem ecclesiis, quaecumque alimentum et sumptus a sanctissima magna non habent, . . ." Nov. III, 3.

[27] Nov. CXXXI, 7; LXVII, 2; C. (1, 2) 16, 2.

[28] Nov. V, 1.

[29] Cf. chapter III, pp. 19-21.

[30] Cf. Nov. CXXIII, 23.

Subordinate administrators, namely, those who had charge of orphanages and homes for the aged, as well as economes and other clerics who assisted in the administration of church property, had the obligation of rendering an annual report of their administration to the prelate.[31]

There were two exceptions to the general rule against alienation without episcopal consent: (1) Inferior administrators could enter contracts of exchange with other churches, provided that they had the consent of the majority of the clergy attached to their church; (2) they had the right to dispose of possessions which were under such heavy tax that they were really harmful to the church, provided that their colleagues consented and declared that the Church would suffer no damage from the alienation.[32]

Despite the fact that the law recognized the supervisory and administrative powers of the bishop over the temporal possessions of the church in his diocese, there were certain limitations which restricted these powers. As a result the bishop could not diminish in any way the public appropriation given to the Church for the aid of the poor.[33] In order to insure the proper administration of ecclesiastical property Roman law decreed that bishops should not marry, lest there be the temptation to divert ecclesiastical possessions to their families and relatives. They were also forbidden to bequeath to relatives anything which they had acquired after their entrance into office and by virtue of that office.[34] The consent of the bishop to the perpetual or long term leasing of church property had to be based on the assurance that no harm would come to the property.[35] The solemnities required for alienations [36] and the severe penalties inflicted on those who presumed to violate the laws relating to alienations [37] insured the proper administration of the possessions of the Church as something sacred and thereby con-

[31] C. (1, 3) 41, 11; Nov. CXXIII, 23.
[32] Nov. CXX, 7, 1.
[33] C. (1, 2) 12, 2.
[34] C. (1, 3) 41, 2-6, 11; Nov. VI, 1.
[35] Nov. CXX, 6, 2.
[36] Nov. CXX, 6, 7; VII, 1.
[37] C. (1, 2) 14, 4, 5; Nov. VII, 1, 7, 8.

tinued the old Roman tradition that "*res sacrae*" were not at the disposal of private individuals.[38]

Article 2. Diocesan Economes in Roman Law

While by law the bishop was the principal administrator of ecclesiastical property, nevertheless the actual exercise of this duty in all its details became manifestly impossible as the number of churches increased. Moreover, due to his arduous tasks which concerned the spiritual welfare of the people, the bishop required an assistant who could take care of the actual administration of the temporal possessions of the church.

Mention of such an official, called the *econome*, is made in Roman law toward the close of the fourth century in connection with his obligation to restore property which he had acquired by fraud.[39] In 434 the Emperor Theodosius II declared that those economes who in the name of their church received property from clerics who were orphans and childless would not thereby be liable to civil prosecution.[40]

In the law of Justinian economes were mentioned much more frequently and their rights and duties were described much more in detail. They could enter contracts by which another gained the usufruct of church property, provided that the dominion over the property remained with the church as well as the ownership of the fruits which the other party had received and possessed at the time of his death.[41] They were to distribute the bequests which had been left to the poor, if the donor had not specified the beneficiaries in person and if there were in the city no charitable institutions which could administer such unspecified bequests.[42] Their chief duty with regard to the disbursement of church money was to take care of the

[38] Sohm-Ledlie, *Institutes of Roman Law*, p. 189.

[39] "Sed etiam hi, quos economos vocant, hoc est, qui ecclesiasticas consuerunt tractare rationes, ad eam debiti vel publici vel privati redhibitionem amota dilatione cogantur, in qua eos obnoxios esse constiterit, etc."—C. Th., IX, 45, 3.

[40] C. Th., V, 3, 1.

[41] C. (1, 2) 14, 9.

[42] C. (1, 3) 48, 3, 6.

expenses of the divine service. Whatever remained over and above was to be given to the people who were truly in need.[43] This distributive power did not extend to the immovable property of the church. Such property was under the care of the econome, it is true, but only insofar as the cultivation of the land and the improvement of the property required his attention. His ordinary power did not include the alienation of property; [44] in fact, if he did alienate the possessions of the church he became liable to deprivation of office and to the obligation of restoring the amount alienated.[45]

In order to safeguard the administration of ecclesiastical property, the law commanded the econome to render an annual report of his administration to the bishop. If it was found that he had harmed the property of the church to his own advantage, he was held, according to the measure of the inflicted damage, to make restitution. This obligation passed to the heirs of the econome if the latter died before he made his annual report.[46]

[43] Nov. III, 3.
[44] C. (1, 2) 14, 1.
[45] C. (1, 2) 14, 5.
[46] C. (1, 3) 41, 10.

CHAPTER III

CANONICAL ADMINISTRATION BEFORE THE SIXTH CENTURY

ARTICLE 1. PAPAL ADMINISTRATION

SINCE the administration of ecclesiastical possessions belongs to the superiors of the moral persons who own the property, the pope has the right to administer the property of any church within the fold of the Universal Church. This is a natural consequence of the supreme jurisdiction which the Roman Pontiff enjoys over the fold of Christ.[1] St. Thomas Aquinas gives a clear-cut definition of the papal power over church property when he says: *"Although the things of the church belong to the pope as to the chief dispenser, they are not his in the sense of property possessed under full dominion."* [2] Although the pope has entrusted the exercise of this right to various offices and congregations of the Roman curia, *e. g.*, the Apostolic Camera, the Congregation for the Propagation of the Faith, etc.,[3] this does not indicate a waiver of the right itself, but rather the fact that circumstances demand the assistance of inferior administrators. Otherwise, there would be the anomalous and absurd condition in which a local pastor would be above his superior, at least in his limited sphere of jurisdiction. In such a hypothesis the power of the pontiff would not be full, supreme and immediate over all in the Church; he would not have the "plenitude of power" which Christ gave to His vicar on earth.[4]

It is quite probable that in the very early ages of the Church the pope did not directly exercise his supreme power over the temporal possessions of the diocesan churches, but rather left this entirely in

[1] Cf. can. 218, §§ 1-2; can. 1518.

[2] *Summa*, IIa, IIae, q. 100, art. 1, ad 7.

[3] Wernz, *Ius Decretalium*, III, n. 150.

[4] Hirschel, "Eigenthum am katholischen Kirchengute," *Archiv für katholisches Kirchenrecht*, XXXIV (1875), 310.

the hands of the bishops who had full power in the administration of them.[5] In an age when persecution was preventing the expansion of the Christian religion, the collection and distribution of alms was probably the most important function of ecclesiastical administrators. With the freedom of religious worship after the time of Constantine the growth and spread of the Church rendered impossible the direct application of revenues to the needy by the pontiff even in the city of Rome. Instead, the temporal administration of the pontiffs showed itself directive rather than executive. Thus, toward the end of the fifth century Pope Simplicius (468-483), after depriving a certain Gaudentius of his right to ordain because of the fact that he had administered sacred orders against the law of the Church, also obliged him to restore three-quarters of the income which he had received from the faithful. He decreed that the three-quarters should be distributed equally to the clergy, to the maintenance fund of the church and to the relief of the poor in accordance with the established rule that the offerings of the faithful should be divided into four parts, one for the clergy, one for support of the church, one for the bishop and one for the poor. Gaudentius was commanded to make this division not only of the current income but also of the entire income of the three preceding years.[6] In the year 494 Pope Gelasius again commanded the observance of this four-way division and applied it to the stabilized income as well as to the free-will offerings of the faithful.[7] It seems that these two decrees were the first definite universal legislation commanding the equal distribution of church revenues to the bishop, the clergy, the poor and the maintenance fund of the church. Later, in the fourth and sixth Roman synods, Pope Symmachus defined the powers of the bishop in the alienation of property as well as the causes required for such an act.[8]

[5] Gosselin-Kelley, *The Power of the Pope* (Baltimore, 1853), I, 33.

[6] Epistle III—J. Mansi, *Sacrorum Conciliorum Nova et Amplissima Collectio*, VII, 973-974; c. 28, C. XII, q. 2.

[7] Epistle XIV, decree XXVII—A. Thiel, *Epistolae Romanorum Pontificum Genuinae*, Brunsbergae, 1868; *MPL*, LIX, 561; c. 27, C. XII, q. 2.

[8] IV Roman Council (502), c. 4—Mansi, VIII, 267; VI Roman Synod (504), c. 7—Hardouin, II, 990.

Thus only late in the first five centuries is there found any legislation which clearly reveals the universal administrative power of the papacy.

Article 2. Episcopal Administration

In the very beginning of the Church the work of property administration was a part of the ministerial activity. St. John relates the fact that Judas was in charge of the temporal affairs of our Lord and of the Apostles, for it was he "who had the purse and carried the things that were put therein." [9] His functions are seen from the words of John in the following chapter of the Gospel: "For some thought that Jesus had said to him: 'Buy those things which we have need of for the festival day,' or that he should give something to the poor." [10] St. Augustine in commenting on this gospel said that this shows that our Lord kept a purse containing the contributions of the faithful in order that the needy might receive aid and not be driven from the path of justice through fear of starvation.[11]

This generosity of the faithful was imitated after our Lord's resurrection. St. Paul exhorted the people to see to it that the resources of the Church would be adequate to take care of those widows who were in dire need and without any other means of support.[12] The relief of the poor and helpless became so important an item in the everyday work of the Apostles that seven deacons were appointed to administer the contributions of the more wealthy in behalf of the poor.[13] So widespread was this work of charity and so spontaneous its manifestation in the relief of the needy, whether they were in exile, in mines or in prison, that the enemies of the Christians were forced to testify to the remarkable love which the Christians bore one another.[14] That these distributions were not

[9] John xii. 6.

[10] John xiii. 29.

[11] Tractatus LXII, *In Evangel. Joann.—MPL,* XXXV, 1803.

[12] 1 Tim. v. 16.

[13] Acts vi. 1-5; Reid, "The Organization of the Church"—*The Cambridge Medieval History* (8 vols., New York: Macmillan, 1936), I, 148.

[14] Tertullian, *Apologeticus Adversus Gentes pro Christianis,* c. XXXIX—*MPL,* I, 470-71.

merely individual donations, but resources drawn from a common treasury, the same author testifies.[15]

As the Church expanded its influence, the bishops succeeded the Apostles and collected the offerings for the care of the poor.[16] So complete a charge over the temporal means of the church did the bishop have that once a month he distributed living expenses to the priests and clergy of his territory, since as yet there was no parochial administration separate from that of the bishop's church.[17] In fact, so extensive was his power that he was subject to no regulation apart from the voice of conscience.[18]

In those early years, when the dioceses were not large, it was at least possible for a bishop to maintain personal control of the financial administration within his territory. Certainly it was much better that he do so, because in the times of persecution relief work was a tremendous item and needed the careful supervision of him to whom was entrusted the spiritual and temporal government of the diocese.

At the beginning of the fourth century the economic and social condition of the Church was considerably bettered by the Edict of Milan which brought to Christianity the restoration of its property and full legal recognition.[19] Since then, the Church could hold property legally, it can readily be assumed that the charity of the faithful increased the reserve fund of the individual churches. There was no immediate need to dispose of donations as soon as they were given, and the Church like any other organization could lay aside money for future needs. In the legislation of the fourth century, the bishop was still recognized as the supreme administrator of the possessions of his diocese,[20] so much so indeed, that if any

15 *Ad Martyres*, cap. I—*MPL*, I, 619.

16 G. Phillips, *Compendium Juris Ecclesiastici* (ed. F. Vering, Ratisbonae, 1875), L. III, parag. 202, p. 403.

17 Cyprian, *Ep. 28*—*MPL*, IV, 502.

18 *Canones Apostolorum*, c. 37—Mansi, I, 38; L. Thomassinus, *Nova et Vetus Ecclesiae Disciplina circa Beneficia et Beneficiarios* (10 vols., Magontiaci, 1787), Pars III, lib. II, c. 13, n. 12.

19 H. M. Gwatkin, "Constantine and His City," *Cambridge Medieval History*, I, 6.

20 *Canones Apostolorum*, c. 40—Mansi, I, 38.

other cleric sold ecclesiastical goods without episcopal permission the prelate had the power to revoke that contract or to change its terms as he saw fit.[21] So strict was this legislation that if anyone gave or received church property without the knowledge of the bishop or his delegate, the one so involved in the deal was anathematized.[22] This supreme power of the bishops, however, left the way open to possible abuses of their power, because there was the temptation for prelates to use some of the church property for themselves and their relatives. For that reason it was decreed that this was prohibited unless the bishop and his relatives were poor. In that case they could share the surplus goods of the church according to their need.[23] Despite the spread of Christianity from the cities to the country districts, the supremacy of the bishop in his capacity of administrator was not fundamentally lessened. Previous to the introduction of a parochial organization in the diocese [24] all the offerings of a district had been sent to the cathedral church. There are evidences that the country districts were under the care of rural bishops who were in reality delegates of the urban prelates.[25] These rural bishops exercised the same power in their districts with regard to the ordinary parochial ministration as the urban bishops exercised in their episcopal cities [26] until the Council of Laodicea (380) replaced the rural bishops by calling for the institution of visiting priests to care for the country churches.[27]

The introduction of parishes which constituted territorial divisions within the diocese naturally brought with it a change in the

[21] Council of Ancyra (314), c. 14—Mansi, II, 525.

[22] Council of Gangra (340-341), c. 7, 8—Mansi, II, 1107.

[23] *Canones Apostolorum,* cc. 37, 40—Mansi, I, 38.

[24] The rise of parishes cannot be discerned earlier than the fifth century, and then only in rural districts. Cf. Hannan, "Parochial Ownership," *The Homiletic and Pastoral Review,* XLII (1941), 255.

[25] Eusebius, *Historia Ecclesiastica,* VII, 30—*MPG,* XX, 709 sq.; Council of Nice (325), c. 8—Hardouin, I, 326; Council of Neo-Cesaraea (314), c. 14—Mansi, II, 541.

[26] Council of Antioch (341), cc. 10, 24—Mansi, II, 1311, 1318; Hardouin, I, 326.

[27] C. 57—Hardouin, I, 791-792; Bastnagel, *The Appointment of Parochial Adjutants and Assistants,* The Catholic University of America, Canon Law Studies, n. 58 (Washington: The Catholic University of America, 1930), p. 12.

administration of finances. When the rural churches had resident pastors assigned to them, the offerings given by the faithful of each church were in some measure allowed to remain with the local church.[28] However, even these parochial holdings remained under the immediate control of the urban bishop; for at the time of the Council of Antioch rural ecclesiastical districts existed, and yet this Council declared that the disposal of the revenues of the entire diocese was in the power of the urban bishop.[29] The erection of parochial churches and the appointment of resident priests for the actual administration of the revenues did not change matters. The episcopal right over the conservation and dispensation of the material resources of the churches was not weakened.[30] Perhaps no words are more explicit than those of the Council of Orleans held in the year 511: "De his, quae parochiis in terris, vineis, mancipiis atque peculiis quicumque fideles obtulerint, antiquorum canonum statuta serventur, ut omnia in episcopi potestate consistant." [31]

At most the local clergy of that time were mere custodians to whom the bishop entrusted, as to delegates, the actual handling of the possessions of the church. When the priests died or were removed from office, the property returned to the bishop, and prescription could make no change in this regard.[32]

Article 3. Economes in the Administration of Church Property

The office of econome is almost as old as the Church itself, for in Apostolic times the seven deacons chosen to assist in the work of evangelizing the world for Christ had the obligation of caring for the temporal needs of the churches.[33] This office, created as a result of strict necessity, was no doubt continued by bishops who, like the Apostles, found themselves unable personally to attend to all the

[28] Thomassinus, *Nova et Vetus Disciplina,* Pars III, lib. II, c. 7, n. 2; Phillips, *Compendium Juris Ecclesiastici,* pp. 404-405.

[29] Council of Antioch (341), c. 24—Mansi, II, 1318.

[30] Council of Chalcedon (451), c. 17—Mansi, VI, 1228; Council of Agde (506), c. 22—Mansi, VIII, 328.

[31] C. 15—Mansi, VIII, 354.

[32] I Council of Orleans (511), c. 23—Mansi, VIII, 355.

[33] Acts vi. 1-4.

details of temporal management when so much of their time had to be given to the spiritual care of the people. The prelates of the first three centuries delegated the temporal administration to archpriests, and even in greater part to archdeacons,[34] whom the bishops were ordered to employ in their own care for the material welfare of the widows and orphans.[35] As St. Ambrose relates, St. Lawrence chose martyrdom at the hands of an avaricious Emperor, rather than to be false to the duties of his office as econome.[36]

When the Church took advantage of its new legal freedom as the ecclesiastical revenues grew increasingly more extensive, the need for economes became imperative. This need led to conciliar enactments for the appointment of economes. In the middle of the fifth century the Council of Chalcedon (451) threatened to punish any bishop who continued to administer the revenues of his diocese without having an econome to perform the actual work of the administration. From the wording of the law itself it is clear that this decree was made not because of any mistrust of the prelates, but rather to prevent any suspicions that might arise and bring dishonor to the priesthood concerning the management of temporal possessions.[37] This legislation was but a forerunner of the conciliar and papal decrees commanding the appointment of episcopal economes in the management of the financial burdens of the Church.

In conclusion it is safe to say that in the first five centuries the bishop was the supreme administrator of the property of the diocese. The power both of the parochial clergy and of the econome depended wholly on the will of the bishop, whose control was immediate until late in the period and who employed the parochial clergy at most as delegated economes.

[34] Ferraris, Lucius, "Oeconomi Ecclesiarum"—*Bibliotheca Prompta Canonica, Juridica, Moralis, Theologica* (8 vols., Parisiis, 1860-1863), V, 1442-44.

[35] IV Council of Carthage (398), c. 17—Mansi, III, 952.

[36] *De Officiis Ministrorum,* Lib. II, c. 28—*MPL,* XVI, 141.

[37] "Quoniam in quibusdam Ecclesiis, sicut reperimus, sine oeconomis res ecclesiastica tractatur, placuit omnem Ecclesiam Episcopum habentem oeconomum habere de suo Clero dispensantem ecclesiasticas res cum voluntate sui Episcopi, ne sine testimonio sit dispensatio Ecclesiae et ex hoc dispergantur eiusdem Ecclesiae res, et detractio infligatur sacerdotio. Si vero hoc non fecerit, subiacere eum sacris canonibus." C. 26—Mansi, VI, 1230.

CHAPTER IV

CANONICAL ADMINISTRATION FROM THE SIXTH CENTURY TO THE DECRETALS OF GREGORY IX

ARTICLE 1. PAPAL ADMINISTRATION

THE exercise of administrative rights over ecclesiastical property which the Holy See had used so infrequently in the earlier centuries was decidedly increased at the beginning of the sixth century. In the year 535 Agapitus I ordered the removal of a bishop from the temporal administration of his diocese and commanded the Archbishop to appoint an econome to handle that part of the diocesan administration.[1] About twenty years later Pope Pelagius I safeguarded the administration of ecclesiastical property by demanding that a certain newly appointed bishop of Syracuse submit an inventory of his possessions before entering the episcopal state. In addition, since the people insisted strongly on the choice of a married man, Pelagius demanded from him the promise that none of the church property should be diverted to the support of his family.[2] In order to prevent any financial tyranny by bishops this same pope restricted the amount of the *cathedraticum* which the prelates could demand from each parish.[3]

In this period of Church History no pontiff showed more interest in the financial condition of local churches than did Gregory the Great. In fact, John the Deacon refers to him as an *Argus luminosissimus,* whose eyes were forever looking over the entire extent of the Church in an effort the better to superintend the activities of his ecclesiastical procurators and their administration of the patrimonies.[4] In filling the episcopal see of Fondi, Gregory insisted that

[1] *Rescriptum ad Caesarium*—Hardouin, II, 1180.

[2] *Epistola ad Cethegum*—Mansi, IX, 734.

[3] Cfr. c. 4, C. X, q. 3; Jaffé, *Regesta Pontificum Romanorum ab condita Ecclesia ad annum post Christum natum MCXCVIII* (2 vols., Lipsiae, 1881), n. 700.

[4] *Sancti Gregorii Magni Vita,* Lib. II, n. 55—*MPL,* LXXV, 112.

Agnellus have the fullest power over the possessions of that church.[5] He appointed a priest, Candidus, as the econome of the Roman Church in Gaul with the obligation to obtain the restitution of stolen church property.[6] When Januarius, the Metropolitan of Sardinia, had failed to care for the material welfare of its hospitals, Gregory designated an archpriest to prevent such neglect in the future.[7]

At this time the Holy See possessed numerous patrimonies in Italy, Sardinia, Spain, Gaul, and Africa. Some of them were estates paying annual rents, and others were real principalities, sometimes including entire cities and provinces, in which the pope exercised, through officers appointed by himself, all the rights of a temporal sovereign.[8] To care properly for these possessions it was necessary to have various minor officials, *v. g.*, the *primicerius* and the *arcarius*, whose respective duties were to care for the collection of revenues and the upkeep of the patrimonies.[9] The city of Rome was itself divided into seven deaconries over which presided an Archdeacon who was called the vicar of the pope in temporal affairs.[10]

The offerings of the faithful were augmented after the eighth century by the payment of a tax known as Peterspence, which originated in England. The purpose of the tax was to meet the expenses necessary in Rome for the relief of the poor and the upkeep of the churches.[11]

Although in the administration of the patrimonies a delegated rector of the pope collected the revenues, made expenditures, and periodically rendered an account of his management to the papal treasurer,[12] at times the popes personally granted leases of papal

[5] *Ad Agnellum Episcopum—MPL,* LXXVII, 615.

[6] Liber VI, Ep. 5, 7, 55—*MPL,* LXXVII, 797, 799, 839.

[7] Liber XIV, Ep. 2—*MPL,* LXXVII, 1304.

[8] Gosselin—Kelley, *The Power of the Pope,* I, 116-17.

[9] Gelasius, *Rescriptum ad Episcopum Angoli—MPL,* LXIX, 417; cf. Horace K. Mann, *The Lives of the Popes* (St. Louis: Herder, 1925), VI, 102-104.

[10] Mann, *loc. cit.*

[11] H. Thurston, "Peterspence," *Catholic Encyclopedia,* XI, 774; *Epistle of Leo III to King Kenulf—Councils and Ecclesiastical Documents Relating to Great Britain and Ireland* (ed. Haddan-Stubbs, 3 vols., Oxford, 1871), III, 445.

[12] *MPL,* LXIX, 417—Fragment of a letter of Pope Pelagius I to the subdeacon Melleus, who had been entrusted with the care of one of the patrimonies.

farms in return for a certain annual rent. Gregory II in the year 725 granted such a lease to a certain priest Stephen, who desired a papal farm in Campagna.[13]

In the succeeding centuries the right of the papacy to administer the property of the Church continued to develop in many different forms of control.

A. *Exemption of Local Church Property and Monasteries from Episcopal Taxation*

With the feudalization of the estates of the Church in the latter half of the ninth century [14] the local administrative organization lost its efficiency. The increasing power of the nobles and the lease of papal estates in such a way that most of the revenues fell to the lessees, who became practically feudal lords,[15] so impoverished the papacy that with the additional usurpations of the secular princes it was almost bankrupt.[16]

To meet the financial obligations of papal administration new methods of acquiring income were devised. In return for offerings made by monasteries to the Holy See, the latter granted to the monasteries exemption from episcopal taxation. In the year 867 Pope Nichols I acknowledged the fact that the property right over a certain monastery had been transferred to him, in consequence of which he granted to its revenues full exemption from episcopal taxation.[17] Although no mention is made of any gift to the Holy See by other monasteries and churches which received papal concessions of the same nature,[18] it may readily be assumed that, in return for

[13] *Epist. ad Stephanum Presbyterum—MPL,* LXXXIX, 528-29.

[14] Cf. Council of Ravenna (877), cc. 15, 16—Mansi, XVII, 339.

[15] Duchesne, "Les premiers Temps et L'Etat Pontifical," *Revue d'histoire et de litterature religieuses,* I (1896), 244.

[16] Mann, *The Lives of the Popes,* VI, 9; Jaffé, *Regesta Pontificum Romanorum ab condita Ecclesia ad annum post Christum natum MCXCVIII,* nn. 3883, 3912.

[17] *Privilegium pro Parthenone Vixeliacensi* (Vezelay in France)—*MPL,* CXIX, 1116.

[18] Victor II, *ad monasterium Fuldense* (1057)—*MPL,* CXLIII, 824; *Bulla Leonis IX Gedulfo Stabulensis Ecclesiae thesaurario—MPL,* CXLIII, 618-619; *Constitutio Stephani papae X pro monasterio S. Prosperi Regini* (1057)—*MPL,* CXLIII, 876-877.

such extensive privileges, offerings were made from time to time whenever the required report of the administration was sent to the Holy See.

Gifts such as this and the consequent exemption of the monastic property from the taxation of the bishop have been interpreted as a circumvention of episcopal rights.[19] This need not be the necessary conclusion in view of the fact that such privileges were given in return for voluntary offerings. Rather, it simply manifests the right of the Holy See to moderate the administration of all ecclesiastical property, and the consequent actual exercise of the right when episcopal administration exceeded juridical bounds.

B. *Papal Restrictions on Episcopal Alienations*

Apart from the actual grants of exemption to monasteries and the imposition of taxes on clerical and beneficial revenues, the supremacy of the popes over the temporal possessions of local churches was manifested by the restrictions on episcopal alienation of church property, as earlier bishops were restrained by the *Canones Apostolorum* and the decrees of Popes Agapitus I and Pelagius I from alienating diocesan property,[20] so now, despite the fact that bishops were in charge of property administration within their dioceses, they were prohibited by Leo IV (847-855) from employing for their own uses the property of churches and charitable institutions which were not part of the cathedral possessions.[21] Hadrian II (867-872) strictly prohibited, under penalty of deposition from office, the alienation of the sacred vessels, unless this was necessary for the redemption of captives.[22]

C. *Papal Taxation of Revenues Accruing from Benefices*

So far as can be learned the first instance of papal taxation upon the income of clerics took place when the III Council of the Lateran

[19] William E. Lunt, *Papal Revenues in the Middle Ages* (2 vols., New York, 1934), I, 61.

[20] Cf. chapter III, art. 2, p. 20 and chapter IV, art. 1, p. 23.

[21] Roman Synod (853), c. 16—Hardouin, V, 66.

[22] *Sancti Anselmi Episcopi Lucensis Collectio Canonica*, lib. VI, c. 168—*MPL*, CXLIX, 510.

(1179) levied a tax of five per cent upon the income of all clerics, in order to relieve the burdens of papal administration and to finance the work of the Crusades.[23] Innocent IV (1243-1254) continued to manifest the fullness of pontifical power over ecclesiastical property when he declared that all benefices and, consequently, the income from these were at his free disposal.[24]

As a conclusion concerning the second period of papal administration, it seems clear that the popes extended the actual exercise of their supreme jurisdiction over the possessions of local churches. This activity points out one clear reason why during this same period episcopal rights over church property were somewhat reduced.

Article 2. Reduction of Episcopal Administrative Power

Just as the papal administrative activity increased from the fifth century to the time of the Decretals of Gregory IX, the power exercised by bishops over ecclesiastical property correspondingly showed a decided decrease. This decline in the exercise of power was due also to the fact that conciliar legislation had commenced late in the fifth century to recognize the rights of local churches over their income.

In the early sixth century the bishop still retained the exercise of extensive administrative powers. However, the increasing number of rural churches made it a practical necessity for the bishop to entrust the temporal welfare of the churches to the resident clerics, who at times did not fulfill their office in a satisfactory manner. Thus particular legislation was enacted by which the bishop was obliged to make an annual visitation of all the churches in his diocese, in order that the necessary repairs would not be delayed for too long a time.[25] Local legislation of the time reveals that while some resident pastors failed by defect, others sinned by excess. The III Council of Orleans (538) demanded the written permission of the bishop, whenever the lower clergy desired to obligate or to dispose of church property. Failure to comply with this decree was

[23] Hardouin, VII, 74.

[24] Lunt, *Papal Revenues in the Middle Ages,* I, 84.

[25] Council of Tarragona (516), c. 8—Mansi VIII, 542.

punished by excommunication.[26] The IV Council of Orleans (541) required that any cleric who sought to obtain an appointment to a church from one of the secular princes must have the permission of the bishop.[27] The same law was enacted by the III Council of Toledo (589), which declared that the bishops could grant such permissions only with the understanding that the temporal management of the church would be subject to themselves.[28]

A. *Parochial Independence*

Although the bishop continued to exercise his power as the principal administrator of all ecclesiastical property, certain conciliar legislation made it quite clear that he had not the right of full dominion. Rather, parochial property acquired a stability hitherto unknown when laws were passed which forbade a bishop to take any revenue from parochial churches unless the episcopal church was unable to meet its necessary expenses. The money was to be left with the local church for the support of the clergy and the upkeep of the edifice.[29] The III Council of Orleans (538) enacted a similar law, but restricted its application to rural parishes.[30] Perhaps the strongest language in this regard was used by the V Council of Paris (577), which declared that bishops were forbidden to transfer to the cathedral church the property of a deceased pastor, even if there were no legitimate heirs to receive the estate, and that such property was to remain forever with the parish church.[31] At the close of the sixth century Pope Gregory the Great ordered the Bishop of Attalia to restore to a newly appointed parish priest the parochial revenues which the prelate had received during the vacancy of the parish.[32]

[26] C. 23—Mansi, IX, 18.

[27] C. 25—Mansi, IX, 117.

[28] C. 19—Mansi, IX, 998.

[29] Council of Carpentras (527)—Hardouin declares that this is the only extant decree of the Council—II, 1095; cf. also the Council of Braga (572), c. 2—Mansi, IX, 839.

[30] C. 5—Mansi, IX, 13.

[31] C. 8—Hardouin, VIII, 552.

[32] *Epist. ad Importunum*—*MPL*, LXXVII, 549.

The additional stability of local church property and the enlarged scope of pastoral administration, which was a marked feature of the conciliar legislation of the sixth century, continued in force in the next century.[33] The XVI Council of Toledo (693) forbade the bishops to take the usual third portion of the parochial revenues unless they used them for the repair of the parochial church which had contributed the money. If the bishops refused to take the revenues on this condition, the Council decreed that the resident pastors should use the money for the necessary repairs.[34]

During the eighth century the practice of giving clerics usufructuary rights over the property of the parish church seems to have continued, for in the early part of the ninth century it was decreed that those who were already in possession of benefices should not be given any part of the customary portion which the earlier decrees of the popes [35] had commanded to be paid to the clergy.[36] Shortly after this legislation Agobard, Archbishop of Lyons (816-840), defended the practice of granting the lands of the church in usufruct, if it was restricted to clerics, monks and the needy. To prove his point he appealed to the laws of earlier councils which stated that these three classes of people were the special objects of the Church's solicitude.[37]

Probably the clearest expression of the growing power of the parish clergy in the administration of temporalities is to be found in a decree whereby the priests are by law given a very definite right to administer parochial property. The words of the law seem to indicate that the bishop is to enact general norms of apportionment while the pastors are actually to administer the property.

> "Quia vero facultatum et dotum ad ecclesias pertinentium dispositio secundum canonum antiquam constitutionem ad episcoporum solummodo ordinationem, et ad presbyterorum disposi-

[33] Council of Rheims (630), c. 1—Hardouin, III, 571; IV National Council of Toledo (633), c. 5—Mansi, X, 664.

[34] C. 5—Hardouin, III, 1796.

[35] Cf. chap. III, art. 1, p. 17.

[36] Council of Aix-la-Chapelle (816), c. 120—*MGH, Legum Sectio,* Concilia, II, pars I (edited by Albert Werminghoff, Hanover, 1904), 400.

[37] *De Dispensatione Ecclesiasticarum Rerum,* c. 19—*MPL,* CIV, 240.

tionem pertineat, toletanum manifestat concilium dicens: Multi contra canonum constituta sic ecclesias, quas aedificaverint, postulant consecrari, ut dotem, quam eisdem ecclesiis contulerint censeant ad episcopi ordinationem non pertinere. Quod factum et in praeteritum displicet, et in futuro prohibetur; sed omnia juxta constitutionem antiquam ad episcopi ordinationem et potestatem pertineant. Quod si quaeritur, quae dicat omnia, procul dubio, decimas, primitias fructuum, et oblationes rerum, et ea quae parochiis in terris, vineis, mancipiis, atque pecuniis, seu quibuslibet rebus, quaecumque fideles obtulerint. Quae omni sub immunitate a tributis fiscalibus, et omni dominorum exactione libera, *sub potestate et dispositione,* ut diximus, *episcoporum, ac regimine et dispensatione presbyterorum* manere debent inconcussa." [38]

Despite the many instances in which the administration of temporal goods had been entrusted to the local pastors, this practice was by no means universal. Even in the eleventh century there were in the episcopal cities churches which had no parochial rights and were administered directly by the bishops.[39] Burchard, Bishop of Worms (1000-1025), in his collection of the decrees of the earlier legislation, shows that the earlier conciliar legislation was not at all unanimous in enlarging the administrative power of the beneficiaries, for some councils insisted strongly on the full power of the bishop, while others declared that the administration of certain forms of parochial revenues belonged entirely to the resident priest.[40]

Particular legislation reveals that even when the administrative rights of the resident clergy were upheld as their immediate rights, the exclusion of the bishop was by no means complete. The negligence of the pastor concerning the upkeep of the property entrusted to his care was punishable,[41] as were the unauthorized acts of donations as well as the usurpation of church property by beneficiaries.[42]

[38] Council of Trosle (909), c. 6—Hardouin, VI, 519-520.

[39] Nardi, *Dei Parrochi Opera di Antichità Sacra e Disciplina Ecclesiastica* (Pesaro, 1829), II, 414.

[40] Burchardus Wormaciensis Episcopus, *Libri Decretorum,* Lib. I, c. 210; Lib. III, cc. 136, 146—*MPL,* CXL, 610, 701, 702.

[41] V Council of Arles (554), c. 6—Hardouin, III, 328.

[42] Council of Rheims (630), c. 1—Hardouin, III, 571; IV Council of Toledo (633), c. 5—Mansi, X, 664.

The sale of church property even for the relief of the poor was forbidden to priests unless they had the consent of the bishop.[43] In all such cases of seeming necessity the bishop had the right to judge the need of those seeking relief, although he was counselled to take the more generous view in doubtful cases.[44] To insure proper administration the resident pastor had to submit to the bishop an annual account of his financial administration,[45] and in matters of extraordinary administration, such as the building of a new oratory, the plan had to be submitted for the approval of the bishop of the diocese.[46]

The increasing power of the beneficiaries in the administration of church property must have led them to manifest an excessive independence of the bishop, for in the tenth century Ratherius, Bishop of Verona, bewailed the fact that very often he did not know how his people were being treated by the parochial clergy, who made no effort to inform their superior of the financial condition of their churches.[47] To check the inroads made on their power the hierarchy strongly endeavored to restore the full control of ecclesiastical property to the bishop of the diocese in which such property was located. Again, conciliar law demanded that all the offerings, tithes and first fruits given to the churches should be at the free disposal of the bishop.[48] This legislation, enacted by a council which was held under the guidance of Pope Nicholas II (1059-1061), not only indicated a strong reaction against the independent spirit of those beneficiaries who acted as if they were responsible to no human authority, but also rebuked the encroachments of the secular princes who traditionally interfered in undue measure with the discipline of the Church.

[43] Hincmar, *Capitularium XIX*—Mansi, XV, 481; *Capitularia Regum Francorum,* lib. VII, c. 27—Mansi, XVII B, 1035.

[44] *Capitularia Regum Francorum,* lib. VII, c. 76—Mansi, XVII B, 1041; Flodoardus, *Historia Remensis Ecclesiae,* lib. IV, c. 13—*MPL,* CXXXV, 292.

[45] *Capitula Hervaei* (868), c. 35—Mansi, XVII B, 1288.

[46] Council of Mainz (847), c. 11—Mansi, XIV, 906; Council of Tribur (895), c. 14—Mansi, XVIII A, 140.

[47] *De Contemptu Canonum,* pars I—*MPL,* CXXXVI, 490-491.

[48] Roman Council (1059), c. 5—Mansi, XIX, 908.

B. *The Establishment of Prebends*

Another reason which was instrumental in the reduction of episcopal administrative power was the institution of prebends given to cathedral and collegiate chapters and to members of these chapters. The chapter itself was composed of a group of priests and clerics who lived in community and were obliged to assist at the conventual Mass and at the recitation of the divine office.[49] Since the episcopal treasury often was unable to support the canons, the usufruct of church property was given to them by the bishop.[50] A prebend in such a chapter was the emolument paid to members of the chapter in return for the fulfillment of their obligations,[51] or—as it very frequently happened—the grant of a distinct home and a separate income.[52] This income was administered directly by the canons themselves and, in the cases where the income of the community was not divided, whatever remained after the payment of the necessary expenses of the members was to be employed by the community for the upkeep of the hospices or property which had been placed in their care.[53] Although no explicit mention is made of the power of the bishop over the property given for the support of the canons, it is rightly assumed that he retained supervisory rights over this property as well as over the property of parochial benefices. The establishment of benefices and prebends for chapters of canons received papal approval in the twelfth century.[54]

Gratian in his collection of earlier legislation declared that the conclusion to be drawn was that the temporal possessions of churches

[49] Wernz, *Ius Decretalium,* tomus II, pars II, n. 767.

[50] Council of Aix-la-Chapelle (816), c. 115—Hardouin, IV, 1131. Flodoardus related that Rigobert, Bishop of Rheims, granted to the canons a common treasury and the use of certain lands. Cf. *Historia Ecclesiae Remensis,* lib. II, c. 11—*MPL,* CXXXV, 113.

[51] H. W. Fanning, "Chapter"—*Catholic Encyclopedia,* III, 582-583.

[52] Wernz, *Ius Decretalium,* tomus II, pars II, n. 767, IV.

[53] St. Chrodegang, *Regula Canonicorum,* cc. 42, 45—*MPL,* LXXXIX, 1076; Council of Aix-la-Chapelle (816), c. 141—Hardouin, IV, 1144.

[54] Pope Anastasius IV (1153-1154), Epist. 29 (*ad Canonicos Regulares Lateranenses*)—*MPL,* CLXXXVIII, 1020; Alexander III (1159-1181), Epist. 232—*MPL,* CC, 281; cf. also c. 2, X, *de concessione praebendae et ecclesiae non vacantis,* III, 8.

were under the control of the bishops [55] not in the sense of their full dominion over them but rather after the fashion of property entrusted to their care and, therefore, were to be disposed of only if that was necessary or useful for the welfare of the church and its members.[56] However, the establishment of benefices and prebends, which conciliar and papal legislation sanctioned, leads to the belief that in the six centuries preceding the Decretals of Pope Gregory IX (1227-1241) the rights of the bishops had been considerably diminished not only by the increased administrative activity of the popes,[57] but also by the greater temporal administration exercised by the clergy residing at the parochial churches. Such a decrease of episcopal power foreshadowed the universal law of the Decretals, by which the bishop was permitted to have supervisory power rather than immediate administrative control over parochial property.

Article 3. Diocesan Economes as Administrators

A. *Appointment of Diocesan Economes*

The legislation of the Council of Chalcedon (451), which insisted that all bishops should appoint economes to care for the actual financial administration under the supervision of the bishop, was renewed frequently in succeeding centuries.

In seventh century Spain conciliar law decreed that bishops employ economes for the administration of diocesan property in order to prevent any suspicion of episcopal maladministration.[58] In the Eastern Church the Council of Trullo (692) found it necessary to rebuke the pretensions of those ministers of finance who thought themselves above the priests in dignity. It was made clear to them that they were in reality the successors of the deacons of the early Church whose chief function, the administration of alms to the needy, was subordinated to the priestly power of orders.[59] How-

[55] *Dictum Gratiani* ad c. 15, C. X, q. 1.

[56] *Dictum Gratiani* ad c. 1, C. X, q. 2.

[57] Cf. chap. II, art. 1, pp. 23-27.

[58] Council of Seville (619), c. 9—Mansi, X, 560; IV National Council of Toledo (633), c. 48—Mansi, X, 631.

[59] Cc. 7, 16—Mansi, XI, 943, 950.

ever, the very fact that these officials had ambitioned to such high position indicates that this office was one of considerable importance in the Eastern Church. Oriental legislation did not consider that the appointment of a diocesan econome was a matter of option, as some prelates preferred to assume, for, if a bishop was negligent in this duty, the metropolitan was commanded to establish an econome in the diocese of his defaulting suffragan.[60]

In the Carlovingian Empire the diocesan econome was an established official. His desire to alienate ecclesiastical property had at times to be restrained.[61] To show the high rank assigned to diocesan economes at that time Thomassinus[62] argues from the fact that at the Council of Chiersy in the year 848 Vulfadus, the econome of the church signed the acts of the council before Rodoaldus, the archdeacon, and before any of the other clergy. This argument does not prove his point because the list of signatures discloses the fact that priests and deacons had signed before Vulfadus, as well as after him.[63]

As hitherto, so now the bishop alone had the power to appoint a diocesan econome, although this right had been usurped at times by the clergy and the people when for some reason or other the bishop had been unable to make the appointment. Such manifestations of presumption gave rise to legislation which aimed to stem and eradicate the abuse. If the office could not be filled by the bishop because of illness or in view of some other hindrance, then the right of appointment devolved upon the metropolitan. But the latter needed the consent of the incapacitated bishop in order to make his act of appointment effective.[64]

The importance of the diocesan econome assumed greater proportions when a diocesan see was vacant because of the absence or death of the bishop. When Gregory the Great invited Marinianus, the Bishop of Ravenna, to take a trip to Rome in order to improve his failing health, he urged him to place an econome in charge of the

[60] II Council of Nice (787), c. 11—Mansi, XIII, 431-432.
[61] *Capitularia Caroli Magni,* lib. II, c. 29—Mansi, XVII B, 746.
[62] *Vetus et Nova Ecclesiae Disciplina,* Pars III, lib. II, c. 9, n. 5.
[63] Mansi, XIV, 919.
[64] Council of Meaux (845), c. 11—Mansi, XIV, 830.

temporal administration of the diocese during his absence.[65] The Council of Pontigny (876) decreed that the diocesan econome make ready for the next bishop an inventory of the assets and liabilities of the diocese. In the interim he was to have full control of all distributions of money to the clergy and the poor.[66]

Due to the increasing number of benefices and prebends during the ninth and tenth centuries and the consequent division among the beneficiaries of the temporal administration, the office of diocesan econome, while always useful, was not so necessary as formerly. Possibly the laws commanding the appointment of these officials had not been exactly and universally enforced. At any rate Gregory VII (1073-1085) directly appointed an econome to administer the vacant diocese of Fermo until a new bishop was installed.[67]

B. *Duties of Diocesan Economes*

In addition to his extraordinary obligation of administering the temporalities of a diocese during its vacancy, the ordinary duties of an econome included a broad scope of activity. According to Isidore of Seville,

> "the econome has charge of the construction and repairs of churches; he is to act as plaintiff or defendant in court suits concerning church property; he is to supervise the cultivation of fields and vineyards; he dispenses contributions made for the support of the clergy, the poor and widows. In all this work he is subject to the supervision of the bishop." [68]

C. *Qualifications Required in Diocesan Economes*

To insure the selection of worthy men for this important office Gregory the Great commanded that only approved clerics be chosen.[69] In fact, so closely was this office connected with that of

[65] *Epist. ad Marinianum—MPL,* LXXVII, 1145.

[66] Cf. c. 14—Hardouin, VI, 173.

[67] *Epist. ad Ubertum Comitem et Clerum Firmanum—MPL,* CXLVIII, 390-391.

[68] *Epist. ad Leudefredum Episcopum,* n. 15—*MPL,* LXXXIII, 897.

[69] *Epist. ad Januarium—MPL,* LXXVII, 1002.

the diaconate that this same pope at times referred to it as the *diaconia.*[70]

Apart from the requirement of possession in of the clerical state, certain traits of character were necessary in the appointee. When Hincmar of Rheims wrote to his nephew, Hedenulpus, he described the qualities that an econome should possess, namely, trustworthiness, sincerity, good morals and strict adherence to religious principles. Above all, he insists that such an office should not be put up for auction, lest greed beget greed.[71]

St. Bernard later expressed a like sentiment. Addressing Pope Eugene III (1145-1153) he demanded the same qualifications in addition to a special ability for this kind of work. Yet, if such a man could not be found, he would rather see this work given to a less trustworthy man, rather than have the bishop personally perform it. In proof of this opinion he cites the example of our Lord who knowingly picked the unreliable Judas for this position. Bernard's words are strong; they entirely subordinate the administration of temporalities to the supreme work of directing souls.[72]

From what has been said thus far it is clear that the office of diocesan econome was of considerable importance during most of the period preceding the Decretals of Gregory IX. So serious and broad were the duties of this official in the diocese that they were to be entrusted to clerics well trained in morals and capable of handling the work of temporal administration. It seems that toward the end of the period here considered economes were not generally used except in dioceses where a bishop had not yet been appointed.

[70] *Epist. ad Joannem religiosum—MPL,* LXXVII, 1137-1138.

[71] *Epist. ad clerum et plebem Laudunensem—MPL,* CXXVI, 273.

[72] *De Consideratione,* lib. 4, c. 6, nn. 18, 19—*MPL,* CLXXXII, 785.

CHAPTER V

ADMINISTRATION OF CHURCH PROPERTY FROM THE DECRETALS OF GREGORY IX TO THE COUNCIL OF TRENT

Article 1. Papal Administration

The more frequent exercise of papal power in property administration, as manifested during the previous seven centuries, was continued on a larger scale from the twelfth to the sixteenth centuries. During this latter period the popes asserted their supremacy over all the possessions of the Church. This is manifest from legislation concerning (a) the administration of parochial revenues; (b) papal reservation and taxation of the income of benefices; (c) papal restrictions on the alienation of Church property by other administrators; and (d) the supremacy of the pope over all ecclesiastical property.

A. *Papal Legislation Concerning the Administration of Parochial Revenues*

The numerous decrees of the particular councils, which in earlier centuries had given to pastors the right to administer local church property, were now crystallized into a definite universal law. The income from tithable lands within the limits of a parish was to be paid to the pastor of that parish. The bishop had the right to receive this revenue only when the land was within the diocese but outside any parochial territory.[1] If within the parish there was a monastery which had acquired by prescription or by some other title a right to the tithes that otherwise would have yielded to the pastor, then the bishop of the diocese had a right to a quarter portion of the tithes paid to the monastery.[2] While in justice he could claim no more than that amount, he was entitled in charity to ask

[1] Cf. c. 13, X, *de decimis, primitiis et oblationibus*, III, 30.

[2] Cf. cc. 29, 30, X, *de decimis, primitiis et oblationibus*, III, 30.

for more in order to supply the needs of impoverished churches within the diocese.[3]

The right of a parochial beneficiary to the tithes of the parishioners was vindicated for him even during his absence from the parish. However, abuses crept in through the undue and irresponsible prolonging of such absences. As a result Boniface VIII (1294-1303) revoked the unrestricted character of this acknowledged right by setting sharply defined limits for its rightful use in the future.[4]

B. *Papal Reservation and Taxation of Beneficial Revenues*

In addition to their legislation which enabled definite persons within the Church to claim the right of administration over specified ecclesiastical revenues, the popes at times actually withdrew money from the local churches for the support of the Church Universal. In the year 1262 Urban IV (1261-1264) ordered each bishop and prelate in England to contribute a sum of money corresponding to their resources and the needs of the Holy See for the payment of the latter's debts.[5] Shortly after the beginning of the fourteeenth century Pope John XXII (1316-1334) reserved to himself the revenues of vacant churches in order to defray necessary papal expenses. This reservation comprised for the first year of vacancy the fruits and revenues of all vacant benefices and prebends which were connected with archiepiscopal, episcopal and abbatial churches.[6] The same pontiff reserved even the income of a French archbishopric in order to finance the organization of a new crusade.[7]

In the fifteenth century taxes were levied on benefices whose incumbents were either confirmed in their office or directly appointed by the pope in consistory. The amount of the levied tax was fixed to comprise one-third of the annual revenue of the benefice.[8] So strict was this rule that the document of title to the benefice was not to be transmitted to the beneficiary until he had guaranteed in

[3] Cf. c. 16, X, *de officio iudicis ordinarii,* I, 31.

[4] Cf. c. 15, *de rescriptis,* III, 3, in VI°.

[5] *Les Registres d'Urbain IV,* edited by Giraud, I, n. 214.

[6] C. 11, *de praebendis et dignitatibus,* III, 2, in Extravag. com.

[7] A. Clergeac, *La Curie et les Bénéficiers Consistoriaux* (Paris, 1911), p. 237.

[8] Clergeac, *op. cit.,* pp. 95-97.

writing the payment of the tax and had certified his intention to observe all the conditions attached to the papal grant.[9]

C. *Papal Restrictions on Alienation*

The supremacy of the papal power in the administration of church property is to be seen also in the various laws by which bishops and other administrators were restricted in the alienation of ecclesiastical possessions.

Because by divine law the Church has the right to tithes[10] it follows that the bishops have no power to grant to the laity the full enjoyment of the same right.[11] If the bishop desired to erect a monastery within his diocese, he could use no more than two per cent of the property of his episcopal church as endowment for the monastery.[12] Much less could he at will dispose of greater amounts for other reasons. Thus, without the consent of the cathedral chapter, he was unable validly to alienate church property by sale, exchange or gift.[13]

In general, the immovable property of the Church was protected by papal law from alienation by bishops and other administrators. So strict was this law that the contract of alienation was invalid,[14] unless the previous permission of the chapter and the Apostolic See had been obtained.[15] Without an apostolic indult the precious movable property, such as sacred vessels and vestments, could not be given to laymen as security against the personal debts of the clergy

[9] Cf. Eugenius IV, const., *"In eminenti,"* 8 iul. 1444—*Bull. Rom.* (ed. Taurinensis), V, 79.

[10] The divine origin of this right attaches only to the right to demand what is necessary for the decent sustenance of the ministers of the Church. The Church's right to a tenth part of one's income is not based on natural law. Cf. Reiffenstuel, *Ius Canonicum Universum* (Monachii, 1717), lib. III, t. 30, n. 7; Wernz, *Ius Decretalium,* III, n. 213-214; Billuart, *Summa Sancti Thomae,* "Tractatus de religione" (2. ed., 9 vols., Parisiis, ?), Diss. III, art. IV.

[11] C. 17, X, *de decimis, primitiis et oblationibus,* III, 30.

[12] C. 9, X, *de donationibus,* III, 24.

[13] C. 1, X, *de his, quae fiunt a praelato sine consensu capituli,* III, 10.

[14] Cf. cc. 5, 6, X, *de rebus ecclesiae alienandis vel non,* III, 13.

[15] C. 2, *de rebus ecclesiae alienandis vel non,* III, 9 in VI°. Cf. Wernz, *Ius Decretalium,* III, n. 164.

unless urgent necessity demanded their alienation by the administrator.[16]

Due to disregard of previous legislation in the alienation of church property, Pope Paul II (1464-1471) issued the constitution "Ambitiosae" by which he forbade the sale, donation or obligation in any way of churches, immovable and precious movable ecclesiastical property and their revenues. Such contracts of alienation were declared invalid, and the persons responsible were to be punished severely.[17]

The full range of papal power, which in practice manifested itself in legislation concerning the administration of parochial revenues, in the reservation and taxation of beneficial incomes and in the papal restrictions on alienations, was expressed decisively and unmistakably by two popes before the Council of Trent. Clement IV (1265-1268) declared that the popes had the right of disposing of all benefices.[18] In the year 1514 Leo X declared that not only the disposal but also the administration of all ecclesiastical property was part of the fullness of pontifical power.

> Et cum fructuum Ecclesiarum Cathedralium et Metropolitanarum monasteriorumque, et aliorum quorumcumque beneficiorum ecclesiasticorum *plenaria dispositio, et administratio, ad nos, et Romanos Pontifices* pro tempore existentes et illos etiam qui eiusmodi ecclesias, monasteria, et beneficia iure et canonice obtinent, solum pertineant, saecularesque principes, omni etiam divino iure id prohibente, dictis ecclesiis, monasteriis, ac beneficiis intromittere se nullatenus debeant: Statuimus et ordinamus, ut fructus, redditus, et proventus Ecclesiarum Monasteriorum, ac Beneficiorum per saeculares ullos Principes, etiam si Impera-

[16] C. 1, X, *de pignoribus et aliis cautionibus,* III, 21. Cf. Wernz, *Ius Decretalium,* III, n. 269.

[17] C. un., *de rebus ecclesiae non alienandis,* III, 4, in Extravag. com. Cf. Wernz, *Ius Decretalium,* III, n. 165.

[18] "Licet ecclesiarum personatuum, dignitatum aliorumque beneficiorum ecclesiasticorum *plenaria dispositio ad Romanum noscatur Pontificem pertinere* ita, quod non solum ipsa, quum vacant, potest de iure conferre, verum etiam ius ipsis tribuere vacaturis; collationem tamen ecclesiarum, personatuum, dignitatum et beneficiorum apud sedem apostolicam vacantium specialius ceteris paribus antiqua consuetudo Romanis Pontificibus reservavit."—C. 2, *de praebendis et dignitatibus,* III, 4, n. VI°.

tores, Reges, Reginaeve, seu Respublicae, vel Potentatus fuerint, aut per eorum Officiales, seu Judices etiam Ecclesiasticos vel quascumque alias personas publicas vel privatas, de eorumdem Imperatoris, Regum, Reginarum, ac Principum, Rerumque publicarum, vel Potentatuum mandato sequestrari, occuparive, aut modo aliquo detineri: ipsique huiusmodi Ecclesias, Monasteria, ac Beneficia obtinen. sub praetextu fabricae, instaurationisque, sine Rom. Pontificis pro tempore existentis expressa licentia, aut eleemosynarum, seu quovis alio colore, aut fuco, impediri non debeant, quominus de illis ut antea libere, ac sine impedimento disponere valeant.[19]

Article 2.

Further Restrictions on Episcopal Administrative Power

A. *Restrictions Placed by Common Law*

Although the bishop's power to administer ecclesiastical property had been considerably reduced by various particular papal laws in the preceding six centuries, the Decretals of Gregory IX very definitely restricted episcopal rights over church property. This legislation, universal in its application, indicated that the bishop was not the ordinary and immediate administrator of parochial property within the diocese. The power of the immediate administration of parochial church property was given by common law to the pastor of each parish.[20] When a parish was divided, the ordinary could not claim the income of the new parish except in such amount as the common law conceded for all parishes, that is, one-quarter of the tithes.[21]

The law of the Decretals gave to the bishop the right in justice to only one-quarter of the tithes paid to monasteries situated within his diocese. Although strictly he could demand no more than this quarter portion, he could in the name of charity ask for a more generous portion of the revenues in order to help the needy churches of the diocese.[22] At times the bishops had gone beyond their right in this respect. For this reason Benedict XII (1334-1342) went

[19] Const. *"Supernae Dispositionis,"* 5 maii, 1514, § 39—*Fontes*, n. 65.

[20] Cf. below, pp. 43-44.

[21] C. 3, X, *de ecclesiis aedificandis vel reparandis,* III, 48.

[22] C. 16, X, *de officio iudicis ordinarii,* I, 31.

into great detail in defining the amount of taxation which the ordinaries could impose upon the various classes of their subjects. He made it clear that although prelates were at the head of the diocesan administration, they had no right to make excessive demands upon the parishes, chapels and monasteries within their dioceses.[23]

B. *Administrative Rights of Bishops*

In truth, the exercise of episcopal administrative power, so strong in the early Church, became subject to considerable modification in the law of the Decretals. However, the increased administrative powers of the parish priests and monastic superiors were not so great that they entirely excluded the ordinary from the government of parochial ecclesiastical property. He continued to retain the duty of supervising the administrative duties of pastors and beneficiaries.[24] This right and duty of supervision enabled him to compel parish priests to repair their churches when it was evident that the necessary repairs had been neglected. He could also demand that the pastors and beneficiaries defray the cost of this work from the surplus revenue accruing to the beneficiary after the latter's ordinary living expenses had been paid.[25] To make for efficient supervision the law granted to the bishop the right to demand from the administrators of hospitals and other charitable institutes an annual report concerning the administration of these institutes, as well as an inventory of the assets and liabilities of the property.[26]

Later particular laws insisted upon the fulfillment of the common law concerning the annual financial report and the inventory.[27] In addition some of the conciliar legislation enabled the ordinary to inflict canonical penalties on pastors and beneficiaries who were cul-

[23] C. un., *de censibus, exactionibus et procurationibus,* III, 10, in Extravag. com.

[24] Van Espen, *Jus Ecclesiasticum Universum* (Lovanii, 1753), pars II, sec. IV, tit. 5, nn. 29-30.

[25] C. 4, X, *de ecclesiis aedificandis vel reparandis,* III, 48.

[26] C. 2, *de religiosis domibus, ut episcopo sint subiectae,* III, 11, in Clem.

[27] Council of Arles (1275), c. 6—Mansi, XXIV, 148; Synod of Clermont (1268), c. 2—Mansi, XXIII, 1205-1206; Council of Freising (1440), c. 9—Mansi, XXXII, 8; Council of Salzburg (1490)—Mansi, XXXII, 502.

pably negligent concerning the repairs of their churches. The expenses for repairs were to be paid, if possible, from the income of the benefice or parish. If the resident priest failed in this duty, the obligation devolved upon the bishop of the diocese.[28]

C. *Increased Administrative Power of Pastors*

In the centuries prior to the promulgation of the Decretals of Gregory IX (1227-1241) the resident priest had actually administered parochial property. Yet in the majority of these cases the right of administration had arisen from particular legislation, privilege or custom. Until the Decretals of Gregory IX had been compiled by St. Raymond of Pennafort, there was no universal legislation on this matter that could be considered certainly authentic. The collection of Gregory incorporated certain rescripts of his predecessors, Alexander III (1159-1181), Lucius III (1181-1185) and Innocent III (1199-1216), which assigned to pastors the tithes of lands within their parishes. By reason of the incorporation of these responses into the Decretals these laws became of universal obligation.[29]

Alexander III had decided that the tithes of lands which were under cultivation within the territory of any parish were, with the exception of a certain portion which belonged to the bishop, to be assigned to that parish. The episcopal portion of these revenues was no more than the customary third or quarter portion which had always been allowed to the prelate.[30]

In the year 1210 Innocent III, in reply to a query put to him by a certain bishop concerning the right to tithes, declared that such income *de iure communi* belonged to the parishes within which the tithable land was located. However, others could claim this income if past privilege had given them this right.[31] Personal tithes

[28] Council of London (1268), c. 18—Mansi, XXIII, 1234; Council of Palermo (1388)—Mansi, XXVI, 751.

[29] Amleto Cicognani, *Canon Law*, tr. by O'Hara-Brennan (Dolphin Press: Philadelphia, 1934), p. 303.

[30] C. 13, X, *de decimis, primitiis et oblationibus*, III, 30.

[31] C. 29, X, *de decimis, primitiis et oblationibus*, III, 30. Monasteries

which were revenues from sources other than landed property were to be paid to the rectors of the churches in which the taxed persons received the sacraments.[32]

While these laws did not state explicitly that the rectors of local churches had the right to administer the parochial income, this latter right may be deduced from other legislation in the Decretals.[33] By reason of this legislation beneficiaries had the obligation to make the repairs necessary to keep their churches in a condition suitable for divine worship. The cost of the repairs was to be paid from the surplus left over from the income after ordinary current expenses had been paid. Such an obligation was certainly a part of the ordinary administration.

Although the pastor could not alienate his parochial property without the consent of his superior, neither could the bishop exchange church property from one parish to another without the consent of the pastors concerned.[34]

Far from denying to pastors and beneficiaries the right to administer the parochial property entrusted to their care, many of the particular councils which were held subsequently to the promulgation of the Decretals of Gregory IX urged them to diligence in repairing and preserving the possessions of their churches.[35]

In conclusion, it seems that although the power of the ordinaries over the administration of ecclesiastical property was considerably modified, they retained the direct administration of the cathedral parish property and the common treasury of the diocese. Their rights in the government of parochial property were supervisory, unless the pastor or beneficiary neglected his obligation. Only in that case could the bishop directly administer the parochial possessions.

could also claim tithes which had been given to them in the past. Cf. *ibid.*, c. 30.

[32] C. 20, X, *de decimis, primitiis et oblationibus,* III, 30.

[33] C. 4, X, *de ecclesiis aedificandis vel reparandis,* III, 48.

[34] C. 1, X, *de rebus alienandis vel non,* III, 13.

[35] Council of London (1268), c. 18—Mansi, XXIII, 1234; Council of Exeter (1287), c. 16—Mansi, XXIV, 804; Council of Palerma (1388)—Mansi, XXVI, 751; Council of Freising (1440), c. 9—Mansi, XXXII, 8.

Article 3. Diocesan Economes and Episcopal Administration

Long before the Decretals of Gregory IX the office of episcopal econome, to which so much importance had been attached in the earlier life of the Church, had already commenced declining by reason of the conciliar legislation which gave rise to parochial benefices. The universal sanction of the Decretals which empowered all parish priests to administer parochial property did even more to diminish the function of the econome in the administration of ecclesiastical temporalities. The institution of such an official was commanded only when there were vacant benefices, episcopal or parochial, which for some reason or other could not be filled immediately by suitable clerics.[36] His duty was to receive the income and make the necessary expenditures for the church. If anything was left over after the current bills had been paid, it was to be kept for the one who in the future was to be appointed to the church. Thus the econome continued to act as an administrator, but only in the exceptional case when a parish church could not be filled immediately and suitably. The only instance in this period of particular legislation prescribing the institution of an episcopal econome was that of the Council of Ravenna in the year 1317.[37]

The dearth of local legislation does not prove that such officials did not function in the administration of diocesan property. Rather it demonstrates that by law their presence was not required. It is quite possible that, since the universal law of the Church did not abolish this office of econome, they continued to function in practice.

[36] C. 4, X, *de officio iudicis ordinarii,* I, 31; Fagnanus, *Commentaria in V Libros Decretalium,* ad c. 4, X, *de officio iudicis ordinarii* (Venetiis, 1696), I, 31.

[37] Rubric I—Mansi, XXV, 601-602.

CHAPTER VI

ADMINISTRATION OF CHURCH PROPERTY FROM THE COUNCIL OF TRENT TO THE CODE

Article 1. Papal Administrative Power

The papal administrative powers which were so definitely manifested by the practice and declarations of previous popes suffered no diminution in the legislation of this period.

A. *Declarations of the Popes*

The Council of Trent in no way intended to bestow power on the pope, who had received the fullness of his jurisdiction from God. Nor did it specify any prescriptions for his acts of sovereign administration. However, it singled out the Cardinals as subject in their acts of administration to the rulings previously made for them at the V Lateran Council (1512-1517) in Leo X's bull "*Supernae dispositionis arbitrio*" under date of May 5, 1514,[1] and put them on an equal basis with bishops in the matter of administering ecclesiastical property. Incidentally the Council of Trent also adverted to the fact that the pope in his administration of the property of the Church relies upon the counsel of the Cardinals. Hence it urged them to keep in mind such a distinctive honor and to so regulate their lives and conduct that they would attract the favorable and well merited regard of all.[2] In full agreement with this reference to the pope's sovereignty of administration, which the Council did

[1] Cf. Schroeder, *Disciplinary Decrees*, pp. 492-493.

[2] "Quae vero de episcopis dicta sunt, eadem non solum in quibuscumque beneficia ecclesiastica, tam saecularia, quam regularia obtinentibus, pro gradus sui conditione observari, *sed et ad sanctae Romanae Ecclesiae Cardinales pertinere decernit: quorum consilio apud sanctissimum Romanum Pontificem cum universalis Ecclesiae administratio nitatur* nefas videri potest, non iis etiam virtutum insignibus, ac vivendi disciplina eos fulgere, quae merito omnium in se oculos convertant.—Sessio XXV, *de ref.*, c. 1—Ed. Joseph Pelella (Neapoli, 1859).

not expressly stress, but which it rather supposed, was the decree that the pope could transfer, if in his prudence he deemed it expedient, a part of the fruits of one benefice in order to provide for the needs of another and poorer benefice.[3]

A further declaration of pontifical supremacy in the care and disposal of all ecclesiastical property is found in a letter issued by Benedict XIV in 1754. While it did not definitely declare whether the popes have the dominion or merely the power to dispose of church property, it certainly claimed for them the lesser power to administer all church property, provided that the alienation or disposal be dictated not by an arbitrary will but by the needs of the Church.[4]

In 1869 the Constitution "*Apostolicae Sedis*" of Pius IX excommunicated those who alienated ecclesiastical property without the requisite authority of the Holy See [5] and in violation of the penal laws stated in the Decretals for prohibited alienations.[6]

B. *Applications of the Power According to the Decretalists and Commentators*

Since the pope is the supreme administrator of all ecclesiastical property,[7] he could impose a pension to be derived from the fruits of the benefice and thus permit a beneficiary with just cause to dispose of the future income of the benefice even to the prejudice of his successor.[8] With reasonable cause he could also change the dispositions of pious foundations.[9]

Although the pope could not give a dispensation from the law of tithes *quoad substantiam,* which is of divine origin, as the supreme

[3] Sessio XXIV, *de ref.*, c. 13.

[4] Benedictus XIV, ep. "*Cum Encyclicas,*" 24 maii 1754, §§ 4, 9—*Fontes,* n. 428.

[5] Pius IX, "*Apostolicae Sedis,*" § 4, n. 3—*Fontes,* n. 552.

[6] Bulla "*Ambitiosae,*" 1 mart. 1467—c. un., *de rebus ecclesiae non alienandis,* III, 4, in Extravag. com.

[7] Panormitanus, *Quaestiones Subtillissimae* (Venetiis, 1588), p. 391, quaestio I, n. 1; Barbosa, *De Officio et Potestate Episcopi* (Lugduni, 1666), pars III, Allegatio LVII, n. 7.

[8] Leurenius, *Forum Beneficiale* (Coloniae Agrippinae, 1704), pars II, sec. III, cap. L, q. 512.

[9] Leurenius, *op. cit.*, pars I, sec. III, cap. 1, q. 398, n. 1.

administrator he could grant remissions from the obligation of tithes *quoad modum,* that is, concerning a determined amount of support,[10] provided that the pastor or beneficiary could receive a fitting support from other sources.[11] If a doubt arose as to whether any individual should be freed from the obligation of paying tithes to his pastor, the judgment of the pope was decisive.[12]

Article 2. Episcopal Administration of Parochial Property Restricted to Vigilant Supervision

The previous legislation of the Decretals and of the various local councils and synods, by which the bishop was ordinarily recognized as the direct administrator of the cathedral and the common diocesan property [13] and only the supervisor of parochial administrators, was not changed either (a) by the later legislation of Trent, or (b) by particular conciliar laws, or (c) by the interpretation of canonists. Rather, it was maintained and more closely defined by the Tridentine legislation and canonical interpretation, and also by later decrees and interpretations of the Holy See.

A. *The Law of the Council of Trent*

The Fathers of the Council insisted strongly on the duties of vigilance by which the bishop was to promote the proper administration of church property by subordinate administrators. He was to obtain from his clergy and also from the lay administrators an annual detailed report of the income and expenses of the church or pious foundation which they managed. Unless a contrary stipulation had been made in the very act of establishment of the church and its endowment, all privileges contrary to this law were abolished.[14] While the Council of Trent decreed that the bishop could

[10] Cf. chap. V, art. 1, p. 39.

[11] Reiffenstuel, *Ius Canonicum Universum,* lib. III, t. 30, nn. 59-62; Leurenius, *op. cit.,* pars I, sec. III, cap. 2, q. 484.

[12] Leurenius, *op. cit.,* pars I, sec. III, cap. 2, q. 478; Panormitanus, *Commentaria in Quinque Libros Decretalium* (Venetiis, 1588). lib. III, tit. 30, c. 25, n. 5.

[13] Wernz, *Ius Decretalium,* III, n. 151.

[14] Conc. Trident., sess. XXII, *de ref.,* c. 9.

in his visitation of ecclesiastical institutes, even if these were exempt, enjoin the repair of churches and other ecclesiastical property, there was no indication that the immediate administration rested with the bishop.[15]

Moreover, when the Council forbade all those who by grant or privilege enjoyed the right of patronage over certain churches or institutes to undertake a canonical visitation or to oversee the work of administration in them, it added that these matters were reserved to the authority of the bishop.[16] The word *"curent"* seems to indicate not the immediate administration by the ordinary, but rather a vigilance over the work of those who were given charge of the church and its endowment.

In its decree commanding the erection of new parishes wherever the care of souls required them, the Council decided that the rectors of the new churches should be assigned a suitable portion of the income for their living expenses. Since this decree was based on the legislation of Alexander III in his command to establish a new parish,[17] the Council of Trent determined implicitly that the bishop had title to no more than a quarter of the tithes of the new parish church, as in all parish churches.[18] Tithes of long-established parishes were to be paid as usual to the churches to which they were owed by the prescriptions of the common law or by the concession of special privilege.[19]

The decree of the Council which empowered the ordinary to transfer tithes and other revenues from a well endowed church for the purpose of relieving the necessities of another church within the diocese is from its very wording an extraordinary faculty which was given only for an extraordinary case.[20] It did not indicate that

[15] Conc. Trident., sess. VII, *de ref.*, c. 8; S. C. C., *Lycien.*, 23 iun. 1725—*Thesaurus Resolutionum Sacrae Congregationis Concilii*, III, 183.

[16] "Sed episcopi ipsi haec faciant, et fabricorum reditus in usus ecclesiae necessarios, et utiles, prout sibi expedire magis visum fuerit, expendi curent"—Sessio XXIV, *de ref.*, c. 3.

[17] Cf. c. 3, X, *de ecclesiis aedificandis vel reparandis*, III, 48.

[18] Sess. XXI, *de ref.*, c. 4.

[19] Sess. XXV, *de ref.*, c. 12.

[20] Sess. XXIV. *de ref.*, c. 13.

the local ordinary had the right to administer immediately the property of parochial churches. Rather, the Council upheld the previous law of the Decretals by declaring that tithes must be paid to the churches to which *"de iure communi"* they were owed.[21]

In addition to the Tridentine insistence upon episcopal supervision over ecclesiastical property and the Council's assignment of parochial tithes to the resident parish priest, there was issued by the Sacred Congregation of the Council an interpretation of the law contained in session XXII, chapter 9, on reform, relative to the rendering of accounts to the ordinary. In this interpretation the Sacred Congregation of the Council stated that the law merely entitled the bishop to the right of demanding an account, and did not confer any powers of immediate administration.[22]

Thomassinus,[23] misled by the fact that the Council did not demand that the bishop divide the tithes of the diocese among the parish priests, argued that the bishop retained the right to administer the property of all the parishes in his diocese. His conclusion would have been indicated only if there had been no Decretal laws to demonstrate the right of all parish priests to manage the tithes that by common law belonged to the parishes. However, since the Tridentine legislation in no way abolished the laws of the Decretals in this matter of temporal administration, the former law must be considered remaining in force. The bishop was not the supreme administrator of all the property in his diocese.

B. *The Legislation of Particular Councils*

The laws of provincial councils and diocesan synods stress the bishop's power of vigilant supervision, rather than his power of administration. The offerings of the faithful, except such as were collected on a few stated days, were to belong to the pastor,[24] who was

[21] Sess. XXV, *de ref.*, c. 12.

[22] S. C. C. "Conchen., " 11 iun. 1591—"Congregatio Concilii censuit decretum d. c. IX (Sessio XXII, *de ref.*), non hoc tribuere Episcopo, ut ipse distribuere possit, vel in distributione intervenire, sed tantum, ut ab his qui distribuunt et administrant, rationem administrationis exigat."—*Fontes*, n. 2234.

[23] *Vetus et Nova Ecclesiae Disciplina*, pars III, lib. 11, c. 24, nn. 6-7.

[24] IV Council of Milan (1576), Constitutio XV—Hardouin, XI, 890.

obliged to keep the church and is adjoining property in proper repair.[25] If "a great part of the church" had to be rebuilt, there was required the bishop's previous permission. The inference is that for the ordinary repairs and expenses no previous consent of the ordinary was necessary.[26] Bishops had to demand at stated times an account of the income and expenses of subordinate administrators. Moreover, they were obliged to supervise the fulfillment of pious bequests.[27] A more efficient supervision at times demanded that the bishop issue general rules which would indicate the purposes for which parochial money was to be spent, or the manner in which churches were to be constructed.[28] To aid the bishop in his tremendous task of supervising the temporal administration of parochial property, some councils decreed that vicars forane should be appointed for the supervision of the temporal administration in various sections of the diocese.[29]

C. *The Legislation of the Plenary Councils of Baltimore*

In the United States of America the Plenary Councils of Baltimore issued detailed regulations which the bishops were to follow in order that the property of the dioceses and their parishes would be properly protected. The II and III Plenary Councils demanded that the bishop obtain an annual account of the management of ecclesiastical property by subordinate administrators.[30] This report

[25] Synod of Malines (1607), t. 22, c. 7—Hardouin, XI, 1692.

[26] Provincial Synod of Benevento (1693), tit. 40, c. 3—*Collectio Lacensis* (hereafter to be designated *Coll. Lac.*), I, 74; Council of Vienna (1858), tit. VII, c. 6, nn. 7, 8—*Coll. Lac.*, V, 219. This latter council required the ordinary's permission for extraordinary expenses which exceeded a certain defined sum.

[27] Third Provincial Council of Tuam (1858), c. 17, n. 3—*Coll. Lac.*, III, 888; Provincial Council of Bourges (1850), tit. I—*Coll. Lac.*, IV, 1098; Provincial Council of Lyons (1850), tit. XXIII, c. 5—*Coll. Lac.*, IV, 481.

[28] Provincial Council of Bordeaux (1850), tit. II, c. 1, n. 5—*Coll. Lac.*, IV, 559.

[29] Provincial Council of Vannes (1859), c. XXVII—*Coll. Lac.*, VI, 343; Provincial Synod of New Granada (1868), tit. IX, c. 3—*Coll. Lac.*, VI, 554.

[30] *Concilii Plenarii Baltimorensis II Decreta* (1866), tit. IV, nn. 192, 196; *Acta et Decreta Concilii Plenarii Baltimorensis Tertii*, tit. IX, c. II, n. 272.

was to contain a detailed account of the property under administration as well as a complete mention of the assets and debts of the parish or pious institute. Should it be necessary for the bishop to examine the report more thoroughly, the bishop could avail himself of the help of qualified accountants.[81] Documents which recorded the sale, purchase or transfer of ecclesiastical property had to be deposited in the episcopal archives. To prevent civil entanglements they had to be drawn up in the form required by civil law.[82] An inventory of parish property was to be made by the pastor. This list was to include all sacred vessels and all other sacred furnishings as well as everything belonging to the rectory, schools and cemetery; in addition mention had to be made of the permanent income and the expenses charged against the parish. The pastor was obliged to send a copy of this inventory to the diocesan archives. Each year the list had to be reviewed by the pastor and trustees who would note the acquisitions and expenditures of the current year. Then the revised list had to be sent to the Chancellor of the diocese.[83] The written permission of the local ordinary was required by the pastor: (1) who undertook to build, dismantle or notably change or enlarge a church, school or rectory; (2) who wished to burden a church or other sacred place with debt; (3) who desired to hold in his own name the property of the church; (4) who lent his own money at interest to the church.[84] The local ordinary had the right to decide concerning the necessity of trustees for the administration of parochial property and the further right to approve or reject those nominated by the pastor.[85] The local ordinary was to supervise the methods used by pastors in obtaining money for their churches and parishes, and his permission was necessary before picnics, excursions and fairs could be held for the purpose of supporting the parish.[86]

[81] *Acta et Decreta Concilii Plenarii Baltimorensis Tertii, loc. cit.*

[82] *Op. cit.*, tit. IX, nn. 270-271.

[83] *Op. cit.*, tit. IX, n. 276.

[84] *Op. cit.*, tit. IX, nn. 279-281.

[85] *Op. cit.*, tit. IX, n. 287.

[86] *Op. cit.*, tit. IX, n. 290; *Conc. Plen. Balt. II Decreta*, n. 396.

D. *The Interpretation of the Canonists*

The commentators on the laws of the Decretals of Gregory IX and on the decrees of the Council of Trent are of the opinion that the ordinary episcopal power over parochial property is supervisory rather than immediately administrative.[37] In their opinion the bishop had no power to transfer superfluous possessions from one church to another. This opinion is based on the presumption that the faithful donated their money for their own church.[38] He, however, could tax the parishioners of a parish as well as of his own church a certain amount *per capita* and compel them to pay this tax for the repairs of their own church when the parish account could not bear the expense.[39]

In the nineteenth century, declarations from the popes and from the congregations of the Roman Curia gave final sanction to the opinion that the power of the bishops over the administration of parochial property was one of vigilant supervision rather than one of direct and immediate administration.

E. *Declarations of the Popes and Roman Congregations*

(1) Supervision of the Ordinary Enforced and Defined by Papal Letters

Pius VII (1800-1823) strongly rebuked certain clerics and laymen of the United States for their attempt to exclude the bishop entirely from the administration of parochial property.[40] About forty years later, Pius IX (1846-1878) in a letter to the bishops of Sicily urged them to supervise carefully the goods of the Church: *"eiusque bona tueri, ac rectae illorum administrationi sedulo consulere ac summopere cavere; ut pia Missarum praesertim legata, et onera*

[37] Cf., *e. g.*, Leurenius, *Forum Beneficiale*, pars I, sec. III, cap. 2, q. 463, n. 9.

[38] Barbosa, *De Officio et Potestate Episcopi*, pars III, allegatio LXIV, n. 17.

[39] Giraldi, *Animadversiones ad Barbosam "De Officio et Potestate Parochi"* (Romae, 1774), pars I, cap. 13, n. 13.

[40] Litt. ap. *"Non sine magno,"* 24 aug. 1822, nn. 1, 3—*Fontes*, n. 480.

accurate serventur, ac religiosae impleantur, etc." [41] Leo also indicated that bishops have the immediate right to administer parochial property only when it was evident that the pastors had not performed their work properly.[42] The extent of their supervision included not only the churches under the care of the diocesan clergy, but also those entrusted to the regular clergy. The latter also were obliged to render an account of the property administration of the parish churches entrusted to them, but not of the property possessed by the institute.[43]

(2) Supervision of the Ordinary Reinforced and Defined by the Decrees of the Congregations

Although the bishop's ordinary power of parochial property administration was strictly that of supervision, respect of this episcopal right was insisted upon by the decrees of the Roman Congregations, which continually refused the requests of subordinate administrators, who, while desiring to be entirely independent of the ordinary, attempted to avoid their obligation of rendering the annual financial report concerning their administration. In fact, the ordinary was empowered to demand these accounts under threat of censure.[44] Privilege, prescription and custom had no force against this law. Only if a contrary right had been granted by the bishop or the Holy See in the very foundation of the institute could exception be taken against the bishop's demand for a financial account.[45] If it actually became necessary to do so, the ordinary could go to the archives of the church or institute whose administrator refused to render an account, or he could command that the accounts be brought to the episcopal residence at times other than that of the canonical

[41] Ep. encycl. "*Cum nuper,*" 20 ian. 1858, n. 2—*Fontes,* n. 523.

[42] Ep. encycl. "*Constanti Hungarorum,*" 2 sept. 1892, n. 9—*Fontes,* n. 620.

[43] Leo XIII, const. "*Romanos Pontifices,*" 8 maii 1881, nn. 4, 23, 25—*Fontes,* n. 582.

[44] S. C. C., *Zamoren.,* 27 mart. 1591—*Fontes,* n. 2226; S. C. P. F., 16 sept. 1771—*Collectanea S. C. P. F.,* n. 484.

[45] S. C. C., *Civitatis Urbaniae,* 17 iul. 1638—*Fontes,* n. 2593; *Constantien.,* 17 nov. 1629, ad 6—*Fontes,* n. 2514; *Eugubina,* 12 nov. 1633—*Fontes,* n. 2556.

visitation.[46] If the bishop rightfully suspected that the administrators of confraternities were not doing their work properly, he could demand that they make no disbursements without his previous knowledge and consent. Moreover, he could insist that they submit a budget beforehand in order that he might learn the estimated income and expense for the coming year.[47]

In conclusion, it appears clear that the Decretal laws which attributed to the bishops only supervisory rights over parochial property, were upheld and more clearly limited during the period from the Council of Trent to the Code of Canon Law in 1918. The Code took over in great measure the past legislation and its interpretation by the commentators.

Article 3. Diocesan Economes as Administrators from the Council of Trent to the Code of Canon Law

The legislation which preceded the Council of Trent had provided for the appointment of economes only in the extraordinary cases in which an episcopal see or a parochial benefice could not be filled quickly and suitably. The Council of Trent renewed the former legislation almost verbatim.[48]

A few of the particular councils after the Council of Trent decreed that economes should be appointed to assist the bishop in the temporal administration of the diocese. The V Council of Milan (1579) under the presidency of the illustrious St. Charles Borromeo ordered all the bishops of the province to appoint economes in order that the bishops might be able to devote all their time to the spiritual welfare of their dioceses. The econome was obliged to give an account of his stewardship to the bishop, who in turn would make a financial report every three years to the provincial council.[49]

A later provincial council at Naples implied the existence of

[46] S. C. C., *Tarraconen.*, 10 iun. 1684—*Fontes*, n. 2881; *Narnien.*, 8 aug. 1693—*Fontes*, n. 2937.

[47] S. C. C., *Iuvenacen.*, 2 iun., 7 iul., 22 sept., 17 nov. 1736—*Fontes*. nn. 3460, 3463.

[48] Sess. XXIV, *de ref.*, c. 16.

[49] C. 11—Mansi, XXXIV A, 470.

economes when it urged these officials faithfully to fulfill their duties. However, the council in no way commanded that they be appointed in each diocese.[50]

In the United States two of the councils of Baltimore desired the appointment of episcopal economes to care for all ecclesiastical property of their diocese and especially to supervise the business transactions of nuns. Laymen could be appointed to this office, and had the obligation of rendering an annual account of their administration to the local ordinary.[51]

In conclusion, it appears that during the centuries from the Council of Trent to the Code of Canon Law, economes were demanded by the common law only when a diocese or parish was vacant. Particular laws of this period, however, decreed their appointment for the greater temporal and spiritual welfare of the diocese.

[50] Provincial Synod of Naples (1699), tit. II, n. 12—*Coll. Lac.,* I, 167.

[51] *II Plen. Conc. Baltimorense* (1866), tit. II, c. 5, n. 75; tit. IV, n. 196; *X Prov. Conc. Baltimorense* (1869)—*Coll. Lac.,* III, 589.

PART TWO

CANONICAL COMMENTARY

CHAPTER VII

THE POPE AS THE ADMINISTRATOR OF ECCLESIASTICAL PROPERTY

THE historical synopsis of the administration of church property has shown that the Church has entrusted this work of administration to many individuals. Just as there is a hierarchical order of jurisdiction in general, so too in that part of jurisdictional power which is concerned with the property of the Church there is a systematic subordination of inferior to superior. Since the Roman Pontiff has supreme jurisdiction over all people and all property within the Universal Church [1] and since the right to administer property is part of the executive power which flows from jurisdiction,[2] the Code of Canon Law very aptly declares that the pope is the supreme administrator and dispenser of ecclesiastical property "*Romanus Pontifex est omnium bonorum ecclesiasticorum supremus administrator et dispensator.*" [3]

ARTICLE 1. NATURE AND EXTENT OF PAPAL ADMINISTRATIVE POWER

The pope's power is said to be supreme, that is, it is declared to be the right to administer immediately and mediately any ecclesiastical property whatever. In this respect it differs from the administrative right of any other bishop, who cannot claim for himself a like power of immediate as well as mediate administration over all church property in his diocese. *Immediate* administration means the direct management of ecclesiastical property. *Mediate* administration signifies the indirect management of property through legislation.

[1] Canon 218.

[2] Ottaviani, *Institutiones Iuris Publici Ecclesiastici,* I, 120, 233.

[3] Canon 1518.

It seems that Vromant unnecessarily limits the administrative power of the pope to a supremacy which extends only to mediate administration of the property of moral persons other than the Holy See.[4] Such a definition of *"supreme"* would not enable the Holy Father to administer directly the property of subordinate ecclesiastical moral persons. Supremacy must be considered here to include the right of direct administration over any moral person within the Church, because the pope has ordinary and immediate power of jurisdiction over each and every subordinate moral person.[5] The exercise of this power of immediate administration requires no other reason than his own conscientious will to do so.[6]

The general right to administer property includes all acts which are necessary or useful: 1. To keep the property in good condition; 2. To make it productive; 3. To derive benefit from it; 4. To apply, pay out and use it for legitimate purposes.[7] All these acts and more the pope may perform. Therefore, as the supreme administrator of all ecclesiastical property, the pope may exercise all administrative acts without any subjection to rules which are based upon the ordinary or extraordinary nature of the acts required for the care of church property. It is to be noted that this right as such is not based on ownership, which according to canon 1495, § 2, may belong to subordinate moral persons within the Church, but upon the

[4] "Vi primatus iurisdictionis in societate perfecta, uti est Ecclesia Catholica, Romanus Pontifex habet: (1) supremam et mediatam *administrationem* omnium bonorum ecclesiasticorum, in eo sensu quod bona ecclesiastica a personis moralibus subordinatis, secundum leges a S. Sede praescriptas, sunt acquirenda, retinenda et administranda, ad normam scilicet sacrorum canonum (can. 1495, § 2)."—Vromant, *De Bonis Ecclesiae Temporalibus*, pp. 202-203.

[5] Cf. canon 218, § 2.

[6] Pistocchi, *De Bonis Ecclesiae Temporalibus*, p. 71; Vermeersch-Creusen, *Epitome*, II, 520. This power of the pope is not expressly mentioned by Coronata. However, he does imply it when he says that the pope *de facto* does not administer immediately all ecclesiastical property. Cf. *Institutiones Iuris Canonici*, II, 472.

[7] Wernz, *Ius Decretalium*, III, n. 147; Vromant, *De Bonis Ecclesiae Temporalibus*, p. 195; McManus, *Administration of Temporal Goods in Religious Institutes*, p. 79; Larraona, "Commentarium Codicis"—*CpR*, XII (1931), 355-356.

supreme, immediate and ordinary jurisdiction over the Church Universal and all units within it.[8]

The pope is not only the supreme administrator of all church property but also the steward of all the possessions of the Church. In this capacity he may distribute or exchange any or all of the goods of the Church according to his own good judgment.[9] Because of the fact that the pope is above the law of the Code he may alienate precious goods [10] and all property without restriction as to value, just as he alone may permit subordinate administrators to do this.[11] For the same reason he may lease immovable property even for periods which exceed nine years.[12] He has the power to grant condonations to those who have usurped ecclesiastical property, if they are unable to restore the amount usurped. In return for such a favor he generally requires that the usurper pay some amount to the injured moral person.[13] He may also dismember benefices and withdraw some of the beneficial property without erecting a new benefice.[14]

Whereas the direct and personal administration of ecclesiastical property belongs to the pope without any limitation other than that arising through the dictates of conscience, the rightful distribution of ecclesiastical property or its exchange between one moral person and another presupposes certain conditions. These limitations arise not from any positive law but rather from the natural law which declares that every man is entitled to his own property; and this applies to moral as well as to physical persons. However, when canon 1499,

[8] A. Couly, "Les Biens Temporels de l'Eglise," *Le Canoniste Contemporain*, XLV (1922), 306-307; Vromant, *De Bonis Ecclesiae Temporalibus*, pp. 202-203; Coronata, *Institutiones Iuris Canonici*, II, 471.

[9] Leo X (in Conc. Lateranen. V), const. *"Supernae dispositionis,"* 5 maii 1514, § 39—*Fontes*, n. 65; Benedictus XIV, ep. *"Cum encyclicas,"* 24 maii 1754, §§ 4, 9—*Fontes*, n. 428; cf. chapter V, pp. 40-41 and chapter VI, p. 47.

[10] Canon 1497, § 2. ". . . ; *pretiosa*, quibus notabilis valor sit, artis vel historiae vel materiae causa."

[11] Canon 1532, § 1.

[12] Canon 1541, § 2, n. 1.

[13] Vromant, *De Bonis Ecclesiae Temporalibus*, p. 44; Coronata, *Institutiones Iuris Canonici*, IV, 446-447.

[14] Canon 1422.

§ 2, states that the dominion over property belongs to that moral person which acquired it by legitimate means, it uses the additional phrase *"sub suprema auctoritate Sedis Apostolicae"* to show that the dominion of the subordinate moral person is limited in its use by the supreme authority of the Holy See. In virtue of that phrase and the words of canon 1518, which state that the pope has the power to distribute all ecclesiastical possessions, many commentators conclude that the Holy Father has a power similar to that which in civil law is called "eminent domain." [15] Pistocchi and Prümmer state that if the pope exercises this power, he must have as a reason for his action not only the grave exigencies of the common good, as the other authors require, but also the intention to compensate the moral person which suffers some loss by the exercise of the power. In truth, this would seem to be the case if the pope acted by reason of eminent domain as do the civil rulers who are bound thereby to compensate the injured parties. However, as Blat states,[16] the pope acts not as one using eminent domain, but as the vicar of Christ, and therefore is not obliged to make a payment for the injury done to the subordinate moral person whose property is the object of the exercise of papal power. To support this argument Blat declares that moral persons within the Church derive their power of acquisition and ownership from the fact that they have received their personality from the supreme authority. By reason of this act of the human will, namely, the exercise of authority which grants to a church or institute a juridical personality, the vicarious power of the pope given to him by our Lord may touch things which otherwise could be touched by God alone.

The opinion of Blat seems to be the better one and appears to be in closer accord with the teachings of the more recent theologians, who maintain that the pope has power at least indirectly over all earthly things because he is the vicar of Christ, and can use it validly

[15] Pistocchi, *De Bonis Ecclesiae Temporalibus*, pp. 68-69; Vromant, *De Bonis Ecclesiae Temporalibus*, p. 203; Coronata, *Institutiones Iuris Canonici*, II, 442; Vermeersch-Creusen, *Epitome*, II, 505; Prümmer, *Manuale Iuris Canonici*, q. 443.

[16] *Commentarium in Textum Codicis*, lib. III, pars II-VI, 528.

and lawfully if the common good demands it.[17] Certainly, then, he has the same right over ecclesiastical property which is more specifically entrusted to his care. Moreover, the opinion of Blat has a parallel in the teaching concerning the power exercised by the papacy in pronouncing relaxations from vows. However, just as the latter act of vicarious power requires a just and proportionate cause for its valid exercise,[18] so also the exercise of the vicarious power in depriving the owner of ecclesiastical property demands a similar proportionate cause. Hence the pope could take part of another ecclesiastical moral person's property for himself as pope, if such property were necessary for the exercise of his office as seriously affecting the common good. However, he could not take the property for himself as a private person, nor for the use of his relatives and friends.

The validity of the act depends upon the preservation or attainment of the common good as a result of the appropriation. Because the exercise of the act of appropriation flows not from the power of eminent domain, but from the vicarious power of the pope which our Lord gave him, the pope is not obliged to make restitution to the moral person which has been injured by the loss of its property. The practice of the papacy in demanding some restoration seems to be a practical means of avoiding any unnecessary injury to the owner of the property, as well as an endeavor to remove any unwarranted suspicion that might easily arise in the minds of others.

Whenever it is doubtful that there is sufficient cause for the exercise of the fullness of pontifical power in the distribution of church property, the decision of the pope must be final evidence that such distribution is valid and lawful. This is but an application of one and the same principle which maintained that in doubt concerning the obligation of paying tithes to one's pastor the decision of the pope was conclusive.[19]

[17] Cf. Hermann, *Institutiones Theologiae Dogmaticae,* I, 423-424.

[18] Aertnys-Damen, *Theologia Moralis,* I, 342.

[19] Leurenius, *Forum Beneficiale,* Pars I, sec. III, c. q. 478; Panormitanus, *Commentaria in Quinque Libros Decretalium,* lib. III, tit. 30, c. 25, n. 5.

Article 2. The Object of Papal Administrative and Distributive Power

The supreme administrative and distributive power of the Roman Pontiff has for its specific object all temporal possessions held by any moral person within the Church. These possessions include all corporeal property, whether immovable or movable, and all incorporeal property which belongs either to the Universal Church or to the Apostlic See or to any other moral person in the Church.[20] Hence the pope has the right of supreme administration over all buildings, money, land, books, vehicles, and in general over whatever of value can be perceived by the senses, as well as over intangible wealth as contained in titles to property, letters of credit, government bonds, etc.,[21] provided these things are in the possession of ecclesiastical moral persons. Therefore, this papal right does not extend to those goods which belong to clerics or to the faithful as individuals. In order that the pope may exercise his supreme administrative and distributive power over these goods they must be under the dominion of a moral person constituted as such by legitimate ecclesiastical authority.[22]

The term "ecclesiastical moral persons" includes: (1) all individual churches and territorial divisions and subdivisions mentioned in canons 215 and 216; (2) all legal entities which have received their juridical personality from a competent ecclesiastical superior. Numbered among these are benefices,[23] seminaries as mentioned in canon 99, religious institutes as such and the provinces and individual

[20] Canon 1497, § 1.

[21] Blat, *Commentarium,* lib. III, pars II-VI, 490; Vromant, *De Bonis Ecclesiae Temporalibus,* p. 50; Pistocchi, *De Bonis Ecclesiae Temporalibus,* pp. 44-45; Coronata, *Institutiones Iuris Canonici,* II, 435.

[22] Vromant, *De Bonis Ecclesiae Temporalibus,* p. 51; Pistocchi, *De Bonis Ecclesiae Temporalibus,* p. 47. Although many authors do not explicitly state this, it seems that there is no doubt about the matter. For canon 1518 states that the papal power in question refers to ecclesiastical property, and canon 1497 defines ecclesiastical property as that which belongs to the Universal Church, or to the Apostolic See, or to another moral person in the Church. Cf. also Hannan, "The Local Ordinary's Guardianship of Church Property," *The Jurist,* I (1941), pp. 324-325.

[23] Canons 1409-1410.

houses of the institutes according to canon 531, associations of the laity which have received juridical personality from a competent ecclesiastical superior[24] and all non-collegiate institutes which have been lawfully constituted ecclesiastical persons, such as hospitals, orphanages and similar institutions.[25] Above all the Catholic Church as such and the Apostolic See are moral persons because they are so constituted by divine institution, as is stated in canon 100, § 1.

Article 3. Actual Exercise of Papal Administrative Power

Although the pope has the right to administer all the property of any subordinate moral person within the Church, actually he administers personally only a relatively limited amount of it. A world-wide organization, such as the Catholic Church, must have vast and scattered possessions in order to perform its divine mission of preaching the Gospel to all men. Reason declares that the personal management by the pope of every parcel of property is impossible. Hence the pope's personal administrative activity is on the whole restricted in practice to a mediate or indirect management of ecclesiastical property other than that which comes under the direct dominion of the Holy See.

The property of the Holy See is administered immediately by the Cardinal Camerlengo especially when the papacy is vacant.[26] In practice the pope administers the possessions of other moral persons within the Church only indirectly, that is, through subordinate superiors, who are governed in their work by general laws which the Church has promulgated in such a way as to leave sufficient freedom for individual initiative.[27] Canons 1519-1528 contain the general norms for subordinate administrators and make explicit provision for particular laws which are to supplement the general laws of the Church whenever they require more detailed application due

[24] Canon 691.

[25] Canon 1489, § 1.

[26] Canon 262; Pius X, const. *"Vacante Sede Apostolica,"* 25 dec. 1904, n. 14—Documentum I in Codice.

[27] Coronata, *Institutiones Iuris Canonici,* II, 471; Wernz, *Ius Decretalium,* III, n. 150; Prümmer, *Manuale Iuris Canonici,* q. 449.

to circumstances of time and place. The supervisory power over subordinate administrators is exercised on behalf of the pope through the various bodies of the Roman Curia. The Sacred Congregation of the Council rules in a disciplinary manner the temporal administration of property which is under the care of the secular clergy and in certain cases property which is under the care of religious.[28] The power of this Congregation extends even to mission territory for which, however, the Sacred Congregation for the Propagation of the Faith acts in an intermediary way concerning regulations for the administration of temporal goods.[29] The Sacred Congregation for Seminaries and Universities has charge of the temporal administration of seminaries and universities [30] with due respect to the rights which the Sacred Congregation for the Propagation of the Faith has with regard to the same work.[31] The Congregation for Extraordinary Ecclesiastical Affairs handles matters of temporal administration which involve a controversy or negotiations between the Church and civil governments.[32]

In conclusion it may be said that the pope has supreme power over ecclesiastical property, that is, he has the right to administer immediately and mediately the property of the Universal Church and that of any moral person within the Church. Of course, he has not direct and complete dominion over all ecclesiastical property. The only limitation on his distributive power arises from divine law, which dictates that the property rights of inferior moral persons are inviolable, unless the common good of the Church requires that they be sacrificed. The actual exercise of papal administrative power is for the greater part entrusted to subordinate administrators, who must follow the general or special norms of the supreme authority. The pope reserves to himself only the more important questions of property administration.

[28] Canon 250, §§ 1-2.

[29] A. Couly, "Les Biens Temporels de l'Eglise," *Le Canoniste Contemporain*, XLV (1922), 310.

[30] Canon 256, § 2.

[31] Canon 252, § 3.

[32] Canon 255. Cf. also Couly, *op. et loc. cit.*

CHAPTER VIII

THE LOCAL ORDINARY AND THE ADMINISTRATION OF CHURCH PROPERTY

ARTICLE 1. THE BASIS OF THE ORDINARY'S POWER OVER CHURCH PROPERTY

SINCE the right to administer church property is derived from the power of jurisdiction, it will be helpful to consider the power of the ordinary in this latter respect. The episcopate by divine law has received the power of jurisdiction because its members are the successors of the Apostles to whom Christ gave that power when He commanded them to preach the gospel to every creature,[1] and when He bestowed on them the power to bind and loose with the promise of divine ratification for such jurisdictional acts.[2] This right and duty of jurisdiction was so given as not to limit the supremacy of papal sovereignty but to provide adequate co-operation with the pope for the better government of the Church.[3]

Since our divine Saviour wished that the Church should endure until the end of time and with this in view promised His support not only to Peter but to all the Apostles,[4] the bishops as the successors of the Apostles have the power of jurisdiction which was given to the latter. Jurisdiction which includes the power to teach and to rule presupposes subjects who are to be taught and ruled. The pope by divine institution has received this power to rule over the entire Church. The jurisdiction of the bishop, however, is only a limited one, as determined by the assignment of a circumscribed territory and of designated subjects through the supreme ecclesiastical authority. This is true whether one believes that the right of the bishops is derived directly from God or indirectly through a

[1] Matthew xxviii. 19.

[2] Matthew xviii. 18.

[3] Hermann, *Institutiones Theologiae Dogmaticae*, I, n. 333.

[4] Matthew xxviii. 20.

participation in the supreme power of the Vicar of Christ. In either case the exercise of that jurisdiction is determined by the territory and the people assigned by the pope to each bishop.[5]

The extent of the administrative power which the bishop possesses is declared in canon 1519:

> **§ 1. Loci Ordinarii est sedulo advigilare administrationi omnium bonorum ecclesiasticorum quae in territorio suo sint nec ex eius iurisdictione fuerint subducta, salvis legitimis praescriptionibus, quae eidem potiora iura tribuunt.**
>
> **§ 2. Habita ratione iurium, legitimarum conseutudinum et circumstantiarum, Ordinarii, opportune editis peculiaribus instructionibus intra fines iuris communis, universum administrationi bonorum ecclesiasticorum negotium ordinandum curent.**

When the supreme ecclesiastical authority has placed bishops over determined territories and people, their jurisdiction over these is proper, immediate and ordinary. They are not mere vicars or delegates of the Holy Father. Rather they are *"antistites ordinarii"* of the people entrusted to their care.[6] Thus it is that in stating the norms for the administration of ecclesiastical property the Code speaks of ordinaries rather than bishops. For there may be bishops within the diocesan territory who have not ordinary jurisdiction. Moreover, the Code also includes among the ordinaries many who have not the fullness of Orders possessed by the members of the Episcopate.

The ordinaries referred to in canon 1519 are residential bishops, territorially independent abbots and prelates and the vicars general of all these superiors, as well as the apostolic administrator of a diocese, vicars and prefects apostolic of mission territory and all those who succeed to the government of the diocese or territory when one of the aforesaid is unable to perform his work as ordinary

[5] Ottaviani, *Institutiones Iuris Ecclesiastici,* I, n. 461.

[6] Leo XIII, ep. encycl. *"Satis Cognitum,"* 29 iun, 1896, n. 25—*Fontes,* n. 630.

of the place.[7] Although the Code does not refer to the ecclesiastical superior of an independent mission (*missio sui iuris*), it seems that he has a status similar to that of a local ordinary. His rights and duties are similar to the rights and duties of ordinaries in mission territory which has been divided into quasi-parishes.[8] As yet the status of such a superior is rather vague. The Code does not call him an ordinary. Yet he is more than a quasi-pastor, because he is immediately subject to the Holy See. At most it may be said that he has jurisdictional power similar to that of an ordinary. The Sacred Congregation for the Propagation of the Faith has declared that all superiors of missions have the right to appoint a vicar delegate who has the powers of a vicar general.[9] Hence it would seem that the ecclesiastical superior of the independent mission and his vicar delegate have for their territory the powers which the Code grants to local ordinaries in canon 1519.

In residential sees the successor to the ordinary during the interregnum is the vicar capitular according to canon 432. In dioceses where there is no cathedral chapter the board of diocesan consultors elects a successor to the bishop during the interregnum.[10] If the circumstances of time or place prevent an ordinary from communicating with his subjects, the provisions of canon 429 must be followed concerning the government of the diocese. In mission territory the successor of the vicar or prefect apostolic is ordinarily the pro-vicar or pro-prefect or in unusual circumstances the senior priest of the territory.[11] Vicars and prefects apostolic have no vicar general and cannot appoint one. However, they have been empowered to appoint a vicar delegate, who has practically the same power as the vicar general in a residential see. He has all the faculties given to the latter by reason of canon 368, §§ 1-2, and the duties of his office are the same as those stated for the vicar general in canons 366-

[7] Canon 198, § 1.

[8] S. C. de Prop. Fide, instr. (ad Vicarios Praefectosque Apostolicos et ad Superiores Institutorum, quibus a S. Sede Missiones Concreditae Sunt), 8 dec. 1929—*AAS*, XXII (1930), 111-115.

[9] S. C. de Prop. Fide, litt. (ad Vicarios et Praefectos Apostolicos), 8 dec. 1919—*AAS*, XII (1920), 120.

[10] Canon 427 in conjunction with canon 432.

[11] Canon 309.

371.[12] Despite the use of the qualifying word *"delegatus"* the letter of the Congregation of the Propagation of the Faith authorizing his appointment seems to bestow ordinary power on the vicar delegate, because it likens him to the vicar general who by law possesses ordinary power. Vromant,[13] who holds the opposite view, declares that it would be anomalous for a man to be a vicar of a vicar and that the consistency of the Holy See in the use of terminology is another reason why the term "delegate" would not be applied to one who possessed ordinary power. However, neither of these arguments seems to have great weight in view of the language of the letter of the Congregation. Nor would there be a conflict of claims in case the ordinary dies. In that event the vicar delegate loses his office just as the vicar general in a residential see and the pro-vicar is in charge of the territory.[14]

Article 2. The Supervisory Power of the Local Ordinary

The Code does not describe the administrative rights of the local ordinary in the same manner in which it treats those of the pope. It calls the latter the supreme administrator of all ecclesiastical property, while it seems to restrict the power of the local ordinary to that of supervision, unless other titles give him direct administrative rights.

Although "vigilance" does not always include the right of visitation by the superior,[15] it seems that the use of the word "advigilare" in canon 1519, § 1, implies that the local ordinary has the right to

[12] S. C. de Prop. Fide, litt. (ad Vicarios et Praefectos Apostolicos), 8 dec. 1919—*AAS*, XII (1920), 120.

[13] "De Natura Potestatis Vicarii Delegati In Territorio Missionum," *Jus Pontificium*, X (1930), 19-26.

[14] Cf. A. Vercauteren, "Iterum De Natura Potestatis Vicarii Delegati in Terris Missionum," *Ius Pontificium*, XI (1931), 75-78.

[15] Coronata, *Institutiones Iuris Canonici*, II, 433, nota 5; Pistocchi, *De Bonis Ecclesiae Temporalibus*, pp. 313-314. Cf. also canon 1515, § 2, which implies that vigilance does not always include the right of visitation insomuch as it refers to visitation as a special form of vigilance: ". . . Ordinarii *vigilare* possunt, ac debent, etiam per visitationem. . . "

inspect by canonical visitation the administrative work of subordinate administrators.[16]

In addition the supervisory power of the local ordinary implies his right: (1) to know the amount and value of the property; (2) to demand a financial account of the income and of the expenses as well as of the investment of the surplus; (3) to lay down norms for a well regulated administration by subordinates.[17]

The material object of this power of supervision is the same as that which belongs to the pope for the entire Church with the following limitations: (1) the extent of the ordinary's power is restricted by the boundaries of his territory; (2) he has not even supervisory rights over property in the diocese if the property has been removed from his jurisdiction. The first restriction stands upon the fact that an ordinary has jurisdiction only in the diocese or territory entrusted to his care with the added right of exercising voluntary or non-judicial jurisdiction even outside the territory as long as it affects only his subjects or himself.[18] Therefore by reason of this extra-territorial jurisdiction it seems that there could be some difficulty as to the one who exercises supervision and its concomitant right of directing administrative activity in a case where some ecclesiastical property which belongs to a moral person is located in another diocese. It is true that, if one takes the wording of canon 1519, § 1, strictly, then the ordinary of the place where the property is situated has the right to supervise its administration. Yet he has no jurisdictional power over the moral person as such because its local existence is not linked with his territory. In such a case if there is any necessity to correct the defects of administration, it seems that the more practical procedure to follow would be for the ordinary of the place where the thing is located first to advise the ordinary who has jurisdiction over the administrator at fault and to ask this ordinary to command the correction of the abuse.

16 Vromant, *De Bonis Ecclesiae Temporalibus*, p. 198; Pistocchi, *op. et loc. cit.;* Coronata, *op. cit.*, II, 472.

17 Vromant, *De Bonis Ecclesiae Temporalibus*, p. 199; Pistocchi, *De Bonis Ecclesiae Temporalibus*, pp. 311-312; Coronata, *Institutiones Iuris Canonici*, II, 472.

18 Canons 334 and 201, § 3.

However, if circumstances would not furnish the requisite time for such indirect intervention, the ordinary of the place where the property is situated could even remove those who are actually administering the property in his diocese and replace them with suitable administrators in order to avoid seriously imminent damage. If such drastic action were not necessary, he could command these agents to correct the abuse.[19] This seems to parallel the case in which the local ordinary has the right to demand an account of administration from the superioress of even a pontifical institute of nuns, who are subject to a male religious superior, as well as the right to remove the administrators of the property of the monastery if he does not approve of the manner of administering the property. However, such stern action should not be taken if the local ordinary has the chance to advise beforehand the regular superior concerning the need for correction.[20]

The second restriction upon the supervisory power of the local ordinary affects even the property which is situated within his territory if it be withdrawn from his supervision through the fact that it has been removed from his jurisdiction; for supervision is a natural consequence of jurisdiction. Exemption from the supervision of the ordinary may arise from a special grant of the Holy See according to canon 344; and in this case privileges which religious have obtained before the advent of the present Code even by way of communication are not abolished by the ruling of canon 613.[21] Exemption may also have its source in the general law of the Church, for example, in the provision of canon 615, which states that the churches of regulars and of nuns who are subject to regulars are exempt from the jurisdiction of the local ordinary. However, this exemption does not extend to the property which belongs to the parish as distinct from the church, even if the parish is united *pleno iure* to the religious house.[22] The general law, moreover, respects

[19] As far as can be seen none of the canonical commentators consider this problem.

[20] Canon 535, § 1, 1°, 2°. Cf. Vermeersch-Creusen, *Epitome,* I, n. 610.

[21] Pont. Comm. Intr., 30 dec. 1937, ad I—*AAS,* XXX (1938), 73.

[22] "An vi canonum 631, § 3; 535, § 3, n. 2; 533, § 1, nn. 3, 4, loci Ordi-

the wishes of those who establish non-collegiate charitable institutions and declares that the local ordinary shall not have the right to exercise his jurisdiction over them or to conduct a canonical visitation of them. Such exemption can never include the financial accounting which must be given to the local ordinary.[23] Therefore, apart from the privilege of exemption or from the express declaration of the founder of a charitable institute, the local ordinary has the right of full supervision over all ecclesiastical property within the territory assigned to him. Even for exempt property he is at least an interested bystander who, if he notices definite abuses or defects in administration, will endeavor to have them corrected at least by asking for delegated power; or, if this is not practically possible, he may act on his own authority.[24]

A. *Supervision of the Local Ordinary Over Secular Property*

Before entering upon a discussion of the local ordinary's supervisory power, one must note that in individual cases the property of the parish may be distinct from the property of the parochial church. This distinction is based on the words of canon 630, § 4, which show that the rights of immediate administration belong to different persons in accord with the nature of the church.[25]

The supervisory power of the local ordinary over secular property extends to:

(1) The property of all *parish churches*, even to those which are parochial churches in parishes united *pleno iure* to a religious

narius ius habet exigendi rationes de administratione fundorum legatorumque paroeciae religiosae, de qua in canone 1425, § 2?

"R. Affirmative, firmis praescriptis canonum 630, § 4; 1550."—Pont. Comm. Intr., 25 iulii 1926, ad IV—*AAS*, XVIII (1926), 393.

[23] Canon 1492, §§ 1-2.

[24] Pistocchi, *De Bonis Ecclesiae Temporalibus*, p. 311.

[25] "Non obstante voto paupertatis, eidem [religioso parocho] licet . . . ; sed eleemosynas pro ecclesia paroeciali aedificanda, conservanda, instauranda, exornanda accipere, apud se retinere, colligere aut administrare pertinet ad Superiores, si ecclesia sit communitatis religiosae; secus ad loci Ordinarium." Cf. also Coronata, *Institutiones Iuris Canonici*, I, 825.

house,[26] unless a parochial church is owned by the religious community with strict property right.[27]

(2) The property of all parishes considered as distinct from the property of the parochial church, as for example: alms for the parishioners, for the school or for other buildings which together with the church make up the property of the parish.[28] This applies also to the property of a parish which is united to or at least connected with a cathedral church. The reason why the local ordinary has merely supervisory power rather than direct and immediate administrative power is to be found in canon 415, § 2, 5°, and § 3, 3°, which declares that, when a cathedral church is at the same time a parochial church, the pastor and the chapter have the right of immediate administration. The former administers the property of the parish, and the latter administers the property of the church. Therefore the local ordinary retains only supervisory rights with regard to the administration of the parish property. With regard to the property of the church, he with the chapter has the right of immediate co-administration.[29]

B. *Supervision of the Local Ordinary Over Property Possessed by Religious*

The vigilance of the local ordinary over property possessed by religious extends to the following:

(1) Income from property which has been given to the house of a religious congregation either by will or by gift *inter vivos,* with the understanding that the property is to be invested and the income used for the expenses of divine worship or for some charitable works within the territory of the ordinary.[30] If the primary pur-

[26] Canon 1525, § 1; Pont. Comm. Intr., 25 iulii 1926, ad IV—*AAS,* XVIII (1926), 393, which is given in a footnote on page 71.

[27] H. Mayer, "Die nicht inkorporierte Klosterpfarrei," *Archiv für katholisches Kirchenrecht,* CXII (1932), 478-479. Cf. also below, pp. 89-92.

[28] Nebreda, "De loci Ordinariorum iuribus circa pia legata donationesve tum Religiosis tum eorum ecclesiis etiam paroecialibus facta."—*CpR,* VII (1926), 262.

[29] Canon 1182, § 1. Cf. also pp. 92-93.

[30] Canon 533, § 1, 3°.

pose of the donation is the benefit of the parish or the mission the local ordinary has supervision.[81] However, if the donation is primarily for the benefit of the religious house of an institute which enjoys the privilege of exemption, then it seems that such a donation is not subject to the supervision of the local ordinary. Although the words of canon 533, § 1, 3°, might seem to include also the exempt superior of any and every religious congregation, in as far as mention is made only of religious congregations without any added qualification, yet it is evident from canon 1550 that any and every exempt superior, even in the case of a religious congregation, is not comprised in the rule of canon 533, § 1, 3°. Canon 1550 gives to the major superiors of *exempt* religious the right to supervise pious foundations, even in their own parochial churches. Since the donations in question come under the law here considered by reason of the fact that these donations fulfill all the requirements of a pious foundation, namely that they be (1) temporal goods; (2) acquired by an ecclesiastical moral person; (3) with the perpetual or lengthy obligation; (4) to use the revenues; (5) for divine worship or for a charitable undertaking, it appears that such donations given to *exempt* religious houses are not subject to the supervision of the local ordinary.[82] Moreover, canon 615 states that regulars are not subject to the local ordinary, except in those cases expressed in the law. Canon 533, § 1, 3°, does not mention expressly the inclusion of regulars in its ruling. Since the same would apply to those religious who shared the exemption of regulars, it would seem that they too are not bound by the prescriptions of canon 533, § 1, 3°, which does not clearly state that *exempt* religious of religious congregations are included; for in various other laws the reference to exempt religious is unmistakable.[83]

(2) Money donated to individual religious or to religious houses in view of the parish or mission, and money given directly to the

[81] Cf. Supremum Signaturae Apostolicae Tribunal, *Manila,* 6 apr. 1920—*AAS,* XII (1920), 257-258.

[82] McManus, *The Administration of Temporal Goods in Religious Institutes,* pp. 104-105; 110-111.

[83] Cf. canons 512; 612; 616; 804, § 3; 831, 3°; 1261, § 2; 1274, § 1; 1334; 1336; 1345; 1382. Cf. also Vermeersch-Creusen, *Epitome,* I, 380.

parish or mission.[34] The donation may be in any form whatever as long as it is to serve the parish or mission. Therefore, this supervision does not refer to gifts made primarily for the welfare of the individual religious or the institute. It does extend to donations made to parishes, even to those which are united *pleno iure* to a religious house.[35]

(3) The administration of the dowry in all institutes of women religious. The vigilance in this matter belongs by right to the ordinary of the place where the mother general or the provincial superioress has her habitual residence, because either one or the other is obliged to administer this money. Hence the ordinary of the place where the individual religious is located has no right to supervise the administration of the dowry of that religious, unless the mother general or the provincial superioress also has her habitual residence in the same territory.[36] By reason of canon 533, § 1, 2°, it may seem that the power of the local ordinary extends only to the dowry of women religious professed in congregations of pontifical rank. However, this law deals only with the consent required for the investment of the dowry. Canon 550 and canon 535, § 2, show that the administration of the dowry of all religious is subject to the supervision of the local ordinary.

(4) The administration of all the property of diocesan institutes of men and women,[37] provided that the administration is conducted by a superior who resides within the territory of the ordinary. Therefore, the ordinary of the place where the mother house is located has vigilance over the administration not only of the property which belongs to the religious institute, but also of the property which belongs to the individual religious houses of that institute, if these be located within the same territory.[38] Should the property

[34] Canon 533, § 1, 4°.

[35] Pont. Comm. Intr., 25 iulii 1926, ad IV—*AAS*, XVIII (1926), 393.

[36] Canon 550, §§ 1-2. Cf. Farrell, *The Rights and Duties of the Local Ordinary Regarding Congregations of Women Religious of Pontifical Approval*, The Catholic University of America Canon Law Studies, n. 128 (Washington: The Catholic University of America, 1941), pp. 143-144.

[37] Canon 535, § 3, 1°.

[38] Vromant, *De Bonis Ecclesiae Temporalibus*, p. 265; Vermeersch-Creusen, *Epitome* I, 383-384.

of the religious be outside the diocese of the religious house, the norms indicated above should be followed.[39]

(5) All property administration conducted by *nuns*,[40] as is seen from the prescriptions of canon 535, § 1, 1°-2°.

C. *Supervision of the Local Ordinary Over Property Which Is Non-Parochial and Non-Religious*

In addition to his supervisory rights over property which is parochial or which, if not parochial, is possessed by religious, the local ordinary has vigilance over the administration of property which does not come under the two previously mentioned classifications. This further supervision extends to: (1) Pious wills; (2) pious foundations; (3) property which constitutes or belongs to non-collegiate moral persons; (4) money given in trust to individual clerics or religious with the understanding that it be used for a pious cause; (5) property of lay associations which have the status of moral personality, even when these associations are established in the churches of exempt religious.

(1) *Pious wills.* Under the supervision of the local ordinary are comprised all the disposals of property which are to be executed after the death of the donor if his gift was intended for the promotion of God's glory or the achievement of a supernatural end.[41] The local ordinary has the right to supervise pious wills unless they have been made in favor of clerical exempt religious. This exception stands, because canon 1515, § 2, speaks only of vigilance to be exercised by the ordinary, without adding any qualifying word which would restrict the vigilance to the local ordinary. Therefore, the major superiors of clerical exempt religious have the right of supervision over the proper fulfillment of wills which are made in favor of clerical exempt religious.[42] The local ordinary's supervision over

[39] Cf. pp. 69-70.

[40] Nuns are women who have taken solemn religious vows, or who belong to an institute which requires that its members take solemn vows, even though some of the members actually take simple vows because of a command of the Holy See. Cf. canon 488, 7°.

[41] Vermeersch, *Theologia Moralis* (Brugis: Beyaert, 1928), II, 538.

[42] Cf. canon 198, § 1; Prümmer, *Manuale Iuris Canonici*, q. 448, 2;

the fulfillment of the provisions of pious wills extends to those provisions which deal with the establishment of hospitals, orphanages and other non-collegiate juridical persons, even when they are entrusted to exempt religious.[43] Although simple vigilance does not ordinarily include the right of canonical visitation,[44] in this case the local ordinary may make a canonical visitation of the administrators as part of his supervisory power, because the law of canon 1493 parallels the prescription of canon 1515, § 2.[45] Moreover, the local ordinary has the right to visit and supervise the administration of pious wills which call for the establishment of pious lay institutions, that is, those which have not received juridical personality from a competent ecclesiastical authority.[46]

(2) *Pious foundations,* that is, property given in any manner to some ecclesiastical moral person with the understanding that the annual income of the property is to be used perpetually, or at least over a long period of time, for the performance of pious or charitable works.[47] The local ordinary has the right to supervise the administration of such foundations, unless these have been established in the churches, even parochial, of exempt religious. In that event the right of supervision belongs to the ordinary of the exempt religious.[48] Otherwise the local ordinary will supervise the administration of these foundations in accordance with the regulations of canons 1545, 1546, § 1, 1547 and 1549.

(3) *Property which constitutes or belongs to non-collegiate moral persons,* that is, to hospitals, orphanages, benefices, seminaries,

Vermeersch-Creusen, *Epitome,* II, 517; Coronata, *Institutiones Iuris Canonici,* II, 466.

[43] Canon 1492, § 1, and 1493.

[44] Coronata, *Institutiones Iuris Canonici,* II, 434.

[45] Coronata, *op. et loc. cit.*; Vermeersch-Creusen, *Epitome,* II, 500.

[46] Vermeersch-Creusen, *Epitome,* II, 500; Ayrinhac, *Administrative Legislation in the New Code of Canon Law,* p. 377. In reference to canons 1515, § 2 and 1493 confer canon 344, § 1, which does not limit "res ac loca pia," provided that they are in the territory of the ordinary.

[47] Canon 1544, § 1.

[48] Canon 1550. Canon 533, § 1, 3° applies to pious foundations acquired by *houses* of religious. Hence canons 1544-1550 are not to be applied to *houses* of religious. Cf. McManus, *The Administration of Temporal Goods in Religious Institutes,* pp. 106-107.

schools and other institutions which have a religious or charitable purpose and have received from a competent ecclesiastical superior a juridical personality.[49] The local ordinary has the right to supervise the administration of such institutes, unless the documents of foundation, prescription or an apostolic privilege, have granted exemption from the jurisdiction and visitation of the local ordinary. Even in this case, if prescription is invoked against the local ordinary's rights of visitation and jurisdiction, provision must be made for subjection to the commands and decrees of some prelate.[50] Coronata [51] says that the local ordinary may also exercise the rights of visitation and vigilance over institutes which have not been erected into moral persons, but have been approved by the proper ecclesiastical authority. At first sight the words of canon 1489, § 3, "*aliorum bonorum ecclesiasticorum,*" would seem to deny this opinion. Those words would seem to concern only an institute which was erected into a juridical person recognized by the Church, for only by such erection could property given to such an institute become ecclesiastical. However, canon 1491, § 1, has a phrase, "*etiam in personam moralem,*" which just as forcefully implies that institutes which are not ecclesiastical moral persons, and therefore not possessors of strictly ecclesiastical property, are subject to the visitation of the local ordinary. Moreover, visitation by an ecclesiastical superior is worthless unless he has the power to demand an investigation of the accounts, to correct defects and to give norms of administration. Therefore it seems that the ordinary has the right of vigilance over such institutes, even if they are merely approved without any bestowal of ecclesiastical personality. A parallel law is found in the case of lay associations which, although they are not endowed with moral personality as permitted by canon 684, are nevertheless subject to the vigilance of the local ordinary. This obligation arises not only because the members are "*fideles,*" whether they be in or out of these societies, and therefore subject to the vigilance of the local ordinary, but also because these societies are intimately connected with the work of the Church and have done or

[49] Cf. canon 1489, §§ 1-3; 1491, § 1; 1492.

[50] Canon 1509, 7°.

[51] *Institutiones Iuris Canonici,* II, 432.

will do much to foster that work. Moreover, their work has been recommended to the clergy.[52]

If an institute without juridical personality has been entrusted to the care of a religious house of diocesan approval, there is no difficulty, because canon 1491, § 2, says that the institute is subject to the jurisdiction of the local ordinary. If a religious house of pontifical approval has such an institute under its care, then by reason of canon 1491, § 2, which gives an apparently complete list of the matters in which the local ordinary has supervisory rights, and yet makes no mention of the temporal administration,[53] it would seem that such institutes are not subject to the supervision of the local ordinary. Nevertheless, such institutes *may* have the nature of trusts and therefore in such cases are practically the same as the *"fundi"* mentioned in canon 533, § 1, 3°.[54] Therefore by reason of canon 535, § 3, 2°, they become subject in administrative matters to the local ordinary. Canon 618, §2, 1°, which treats of the relations between institutes of pontifical approval and the local ordinary, states that he has no supervision over their financial affairs, excepting the matters mentioned in canons 533-535.

(4) *Money given in trust to individual clerics or religious with the understanding that it be used for a pious cause.*[55] The proper ordinary to supervise the execution of the trust will be determined by the terms of the trust. If the money has been given for pious causes in a specified place, the ordinary of the place where the money

[52] S. C. C., *Corrienten.*, 13 novembris 1920—*AAS*, XIII (1921), 138-140. This opinion which asserts the right of the local ordinary to supervise the administration of pious lay institutions is denied by some authors. Cf. Vermeersch-Creusen, *Epitome*, II, nn. 812, 865; Wernz, *Ius Decretalium*, III, n. 196. There are other authors who defend the opinion. Cf. Cocchi, *Commentarium*, Lib. III, pars V-VI, 323; DeMeester, *Compendium*, tomus III, pars I, 355, nota 2. The latter restricts this supervision to institutions which have been entrusted to the care of an ecclesiastical juridical person. Cf. also Hannan, *The Canon Law of Wills*, nn. 520-522.

[53] Blat, *Commentarium*, lib. III, pars II-VI, p. 485.

[54] "Praevium consensum Ordinarii loci obtinere tenentur:

"Superior vel Antistita domus Congregationis religiosae, si qui fundi domui tributi legative sint ad Dei cultum beneficentiamve eo ipso loco impendendam." Cf. Augustine, *A Commentary*, VI, 586.

[55] Canon 1516, § 2.

is to be used has the right to supervise the fulfillment of the trust.[56] This applies even when an exempt religious is the trustee.[57] If the bequest has been left for pious purposes in general and without specification of place, then a secular cleric who is the trustee is subject in this matter to the ordinary of the place where the bequest is administered.[58] A basis for this opinion is found in canon 1560, nn. 3-4, which states that the competent ordinary to judge cases which involve property administration is the ordinary of the place where the property is administered. If such a bequest has been entrusted to a member of a clerical exempt religious institute, the proper ordinary to exercise supervision will be the major superior of the exempt religious. This is true whether or not the money has been given for pious purposes which are proper to the institute.[59] However, if the benefactor makes such a general bequest to a non-exempt clerical religious of a pontifical institute with the condition that it be used for pious purposes which are properly, although not exclusively, the work of the institute to which he belongs, it is difficult to decide who is the proper ordinary to supervise the administration of the bequest. Although the major superiors of such an institute are not considered as proper ordinaries according to canon 198, nevertheless since such a bequest need not be considered as a trust in the strict sense of the term, but rather as a gift to the institute for the furtherance of its work,[60] canons 512, § 2, 2°, and 618, § 2, 1°, may be applied. These canons restrict the right of the local ordinary in such a way that he appears to have no supervisory power over the temporal administration of clerical non-exempt religious institutes of pontifical approval. Hence it seems more probable that in such institutes the religious superiors alone have the right to supervise the administration of such a bequest.[61] If a trust

[56] Vromant, *De Bonis Ecclesiae Temporalibus,* p. 186; Nebreda, "De loci Ordinariorum iuribus, etc.," *CpR,* VII (1926), 328; Hannan, *The Canon Law of Wills,* n. 787.

[57] Canon 1516, § 3.

[58] Nebreda, *art. et loc. cit.*; Vromant, *op. cit.,* p. 187.

[59] Cf. canons 1516, § 3, and 198, § 1.

[60] Vromant, *De Bonis Ecclesiae Temporalibus,* p. 188; Vermeersch-Creusen, *Epitome,* I, n. 606 and II, n. 857.

[61] Vermeersch-Creusen, *Epitome,* I, n. 606; De Meester, *Compendium,*

is given without specification of place for pious purposes which are foreign to the authorized work of the institute to which the non-exempt religious belongs, then it seems that the proper ordinary relative to the administration of the bequest is the ordinary of the place where the bequest is administered. For in this case the major superiors of the institute are not ordinaries, and in addition the bequest cannot be considered as a gift to the institute and thereby subject to the norms of canon 618, § 2, 1°.[62] Finally, it must be noted that if bequests have been made for mission work, the presumption is that they have been given to the mission, unless it is evident that the donor has intended to give them to the institute.[63] Since canon 1350, § 2, states that the control of the mission territory remains with the Holy See or with its delegate, who may be a vicar or prefect apostolic or a superior of the mission,[64] it seems then that in accord with canon 1516, § 3, the supervisory right belongs to the superior of the territory where the money is to be spent.

(5) *Property of lay associations which have the status of moral personality even when these associations are established in the churches of exempt religious.*[65] If such associations have received only ecclesiastical approbation without being given a juridical personality, as canon 684 permits, it seems that the property possessed by them is not strictly ecclesiastical property according to the norm of canon 1497, § 1, and it appears not to be in the dominion of anyone other than the members taken as a group, unless one considers

tomus II, pars II, 425, nota 6; Vromant, *op. et loc. cit.*; Nebreda, "De loci Ordinariorum iuribus, etc.," *CpR,* VII (1926), 328. Fanfani (*De Iure Religiosorum,* p. 196) also indicates this at least indirectly when he says, "Si primum [fiduciaria bona quae in utilitatem suae religionis relicta fuerint] nullam rationem eorundem bonorum religiosi Ordinario loci reddere tenentur, bene quidem Superioribus suae religionis."

[62] Vromant, *De Bonis Ecclesiae Temporalibus,* p. 189; Blat, *Commentarium,* lib. III, pars II-VI, 521.

[63] This seems to be a legitimate application of canon 1536, § 1, which makes the same presumption for gifts given to rectors of religious churches.

[64] S. C. de Prop. Fide, Instr. (Ad Vicarios Praefectosque Apostolicos et ad Superiores Institutorum, quibus a S. Sede missiones concreditae sunt.), 8 dec. 1929—*AAS,* XXII (1930), 111-112.

[65] Canon 690, §§ 1-2; 691, §§ 1, 5.

property which has been given to the association to continue its charitable work. The latter income appears to be similar to that which derives from a pious will of which the society is merely the trustee. In this case it remains under the vigilance of the local ordinary.[66] If the property of the association consists only of the contributions which the members have made to further the work of the society, it seems that the members could terminate their agreement and divide the money among themselves if they should desire to break up the association. Of course they may not divide among themselves the money given by others for the work of the society.[67]

The supervision of the property of such associations which do not have a juridical personality also belongs nevertheless to the local ordinary, not by reason of the property which in reality is not ecclesiastical, but because the members, as individual faithful, are subject to the vigilance of the ordinary, who must take care lest mismanagement of property promised for charitable purposes cause harm to themselves or to others. Moreover, the clergy who foster such works naturally want to protect themselves and their reputation.[68]

After a consideration of the types of property to which the ordinary's supervision extends, as part of the same discussion it is necessary to mention here a rather strongly controverted question which has more significance than a mere *"lis de verbis."* Some canonists [69] interpret the phrase *"sedulo advigilare"* of canon 1519, § 1, in such a way that they call the ordinary the supreme administrator of all

[66] Canon 1515, § 2. Cf. also Hannan, *The Canon Law of Wills*, nn. 520-522.

[67] De Meester, *Iuris Canonici Compendium*, tomus II, 500-502; Coronata, *Institutiones Iuris Canonici*, I, 911. Wernz-Vidal (*Ius Canonicum*, III, 513) take the contrary view on the matter of membership dues and say that the dues could not be divided among the members because they have already been destined for a pious cause. However, since there has been no transfer of dominion, it seems that mutual consent could permit the return of the dues to the members.

[68] S. C. C., *Corrienten.*, 13 nov. 1920—*AAS*, XIII (1921), 138-140; Coronata, *Institutiones Iuris Canonici*, I, 915; Vermeersch-Creusen, *Epitome*, I, 514.

[69] De Meester, *Iuris Canonici Compendium*, tomus III, pars I, 394-395; Prümmer, *Manuale Iuris Canonici*, q. 449.

ecclesiastical property which is within his diocese and which has not been withdrawn from his jurisdiction. Such an opinion seems rightly rejected by Vermeersch-Creusen,[70] Coronata,[71] Vromant,[72] Pistocchi [73] and Ayrinhac.[74] Vermeersch-Creusen [75] base their opinion on the fact that various administrators have been assigned to specific units of ecclesiastical property within the diocese, as for example in canons 1182, § 1, 415, 691, § 1, 1489, § 3, etc. Moreover, the law of canon 1519, § 1, does not attribute to the local ordinary supremacy as an administrator. This lack of attribution seems to be deliberately chosen by the legislator for in the preceding canon he applies to the pope for the entire Church the very words which some canonists, as De Meester and Prümmer, apply to the local ordinary for his own territory.

De Meester [76] attempts to elude the difficulty with the suggestion that the controversy is merely a dispute of words and that, despite the difference of terminology, the various ideas are substantially the same. However, terms are the expressions of ideas, and in this controverted point the interpretations of the canonists are quite divergent and as a result capable of far-reaching consequences. If the local ordinary is called "the supreme administrator, but not the sole nor the immediate administrator" of all property which is within his territory and which has not been withdrawn from his jurisdiction, one could make a fair deduction that he merely permits others to administer property within his territory. Rather, it must be maintained that other administrators are so constituted by law that they are the ordinary and immediate administrators of the property which has been entrusted to their care. Pushed to its limit, the opinion expressed by De Meester and Prümmer would allow the local ordinary to become the sole and immediate administrator of all property in the diocese, if he wished to assume that

[70] *Epitome,* II, 521.

[71] *Institutiones Iuris Canonici,* II, 473, nota 5.

[72] *De Bonis Ecclesiae Temporalibus,* p. 204.

[73] *De Bonis Ecclesiae Temporalibus,* p. 310.

[74] *Administrative Legislation in the New Code of Canon Law,* p. 425.

[75] *Op. et loc. cit.*

[76] *Iuris Canonici Compendium,* tomus III, pars I, n. 1473, nota 5.

responsibility. Such power certainly is denied to him. If he should presume to administer all the property of the diocese, his administrative acts would be invalid, except for those which concern property of which he is expressly and juridically the ordinary administrator.[77]

Boucaren in his *Digest* of the post-Code documents which have a bearing on the various canons states that the local ordinary is the supreme administrator of ecclesiastical property within his territory.[78] It is true that this phrase was used by the Rota when it stated the law concerning the case in question.[79] Nevertheless, a reading of the case shows that the bishop issued several decrees in order to settle a dispute concerning the division of money obtained from the civil government and concerning the administration of future income from the same source. This is to exercise no more than lawful vigilance with its consequent right to issue instructions for the proper administration of ecclesiastical property, especially in a dispute between the co-administrators of ecclesiastical property.[80] Moreover, the case also has the judicial statement that in thus actting the ordinary used his right and performed his duty, namely, *"advigilare administrationi et erogationi bonorum ecclesiasticorum, quae in suo territorio sunt et suae auctoritati sunt obnoxia."* These words manifestly explain the use of the term "supreme administrator." [81] Nowhere in the case is there any evidence to show that the local ordinary is the supreme administrator in the full meaning of that phrase, namely, that he has the right to administer immediately, as well as mediately, all the ecclesiastical property which is in his diocese and which has not been withdrawn from his jurisdiction.

Therefore, in view of the fact that there is no foundation in the

[77] Vermeersch-Creusen, *Epitome,* II, 521; Pistocchi, *De Bonis Ecclesiae Temporalibus,* p. 310; Vromant, *De Bonis Ecclesiae Temporalibus,* p. 204.

[78] *Canon Law Digest,* I, 726.

[79] S. R. R., *S. Angeli de Lombardis,* 28 feb. 1919—*AAS,* XII (1920), 90. However, it should be noted that this expression was not used in the appeal trial. Cf. S. R. R., *S. Angeli de Lombardis,* 16 iulii 1920—*AAS,* XIII (1921), 392-400.

[80] Cf. Augustine, *The Canonical and Civil Status of Catholic Parishes in the United States* (St. Louis: Herder, 1926), p. 198.

[81] S. R. R., *S. Angeli de Lombardis,* 28 febr. 1919—*AAS,* XII (1920), 91.

law itself for calling the ordinary the supreme administrator, and in view of the more common opinion of the commentators against the use of such a title, it seems that the use of this term is wrong, especially because of the far-reaching conclusions that may result therefrom in relation to the invalidity or validity of many administrative acts.

Article 3. The Immediate Administrative Powers of the Local Ordinary

Although the words of canon 1519, § 1, "*advigilare administrationi omnium bonorum ecclesiasticorum,*" seem to be comprehensive enough of themselves to imply a denial of supreme administrative power, the clause "*salvis legitimis praescriptionibus, quae eidem potiora iura tribuunt*" shows clearly that the local ordinary can possess certain rights to immediate administration,[82] even over property which is not strictly diocesan. These rights of the ordinary extend to the following units of ecclesiastical property: (1) Property which is strictly diocesan; (2) property which constitutes the *mensa episcopalis;* (3) alms given for churches which are entrusted to religious, although the latter have not the dominion or the perpetual or quasi-perpetual use of them; (4) property of the cathedral church; (5) alms which have been donated for a charitable purpose which is unspecified; (6) the bequests contained in wills; (7) the revenue accruing from the establishment of pensions and the levying of taxes; (8) the property of divided or extinct parishes; (9) property which he administers in virtue of a special title of administration.

(I) *Property which is strictly diocesan.* Diocesan property signifies those possessions which belong to the diocese considered as a moral person distinct from the parishes and other juridical persons within the territory of the ordinary. Such property includes special collections for the welfare of the diocese as such, taxes imposed on the various churches and other moral persons for the same purpose according to the law of canon 1505, and the property which remains after parishes have been suppressed in accordance with the norms

[82] Cf. chapter VII, p. 57, for the definition of immediate administration.

of canon 1501. In some mission territories certain forms of alms or Mass stipends belong to the vicariate or prefecture according to the particular law of the territory and the approval of such law by the Congregation for the Propagation of the Faith.[83] Moreover, money given to missionaries who have charge of mission stations which have not obtained the juridical character of a quasi-parish belongs to the vicariate or prefecture unless it is clear that the money was sent to the missionaries as a personal gift.[84]

The local ordinary is inherently in his office the authorized administrator (*administrator natus*) of the property which belongs to the diocese or mission territory.[85] Far from abolishing his right in this respect, the Code has explicitly renewed and confirmed it in canon 335, § 1.[86] Of course, the ordinary remains subject to the pope and is obliged to observe the general law of the Church in his acts of administration.[87] Thus the ordinary must fulfill the will of the faithful in their benefactions, not only by using their bequests for the pious causes designated by them, but also by administering and utilizing them in the manner specified by the donors.[88]

(II) *The property which constitutes the "mensa episcopalis."* The *"mensa episcopalis"* signifies the property and its income which have been set aside for the maintenance of the ordinary, the ministers of the cathedral church and for the necessary upkeep of the building which houses them.[89] This title of administrative right does not include the maintenance of the cathedral church. As will be seen, the ordinary is the co-administrator in that case.

(III) *Alms given for churches entrusted to religious, in those cases in which the religious have neither the dominion nor the perpetual nor quasi-perpetual use of them.* The alms in question here are

83 Vromant, *De Bonis Ecclesiae Temporalibus,* p. 94.

84 Vromant, *op. cit.,* p. 218.

85 Pistocchi, *De Bonis Ecclesiae Temporalibus,* p. 122.

86 De Meester, *Compendium,* tomus III, pars I, 394, nota 6; Coronata, *Institutiones Iuris Canonici,* II, 472.

87 Ayrinhac, *Constitution of the Church in the New Code of Canon Law,* p. 158.

88 Canon 1514.

89 Cf. canon 1483, §§ 1-2. See also Coronata, *Institutiones Iuris Canonici,* II, 472; Vromant, *De Bonis Ecclesiae Temporalibus,* pp. 35, 92.

those which have been given for the construction, repair, restoration or adornment of a church, the care of which religious have without at the same time possessing the title of dominion or the right to a perpetual or quasi-perpetual use of it. Should the religious own the church or have the perpetual or quasi-perpetual use of it, the immediate administrative rights belong to the religious superior, because such a church is considered to be a *religious* church.[90] From the wording of canon 630, § 4, it seems impossible at first sight not to attribute to the local ordinary full administrative rights over secular churches which are part of the parish which has been entrusted to or united *pleno iure* with a religious community. However, a difficulty arises when one attempts to square this provision with the words of canon 1182, § 1.[91]

The case in question refers to the administration of a *secular* church, that is, a church which is not considered to be a church of a religious community,[92] in a parish which has been entrusted to or united *pleno iure* to a religious community.[93] Various solutions

[90] Canon 630, § 4. Cf. Maroto, "Annotationes," *CpR,* VII (1926), 438; Vermeersch-Creusen, *Epitome,* II, 291; Vromant, *De Bonis Ecclesiae Temporalibus,* p. 216; Nebreda, "De loci Ordinariorum iuribus circa pia legata donationesve tum Religiosis tum eorum ecclesiis etiam paroecialibus facta," *CpR,* VII (1926), 330, for this interpretation of the clause "si ecclesia sit communitatis religiosae."

[91] "Firmo praescripto can. 1519-1528, *administratio bonorum quae destinata sunt reparandae decorandaeque ecclesiae divinoque in eadem cultu exercendo,* pertinet, nisi aliud ex speciali titulo vel legitima consuetudine constet, ad Episcopum cum Capitulo, si de ecclesia cathedrali agatur; ad Capitulum ecclesiae collegiatae, si de collegiata; *ad rectorem, si de alia ecclesia."*

[92] Cf. above for the definition of a religious church.

[93] A religious parish, that is, one which is united *pleno iure* to a religious community, is one in which the religious community has the right not only to the temporal administration of the parish, but also the right to nominate a religious for the actual spiritual care of the people, provided that the local ordinary confirms the nomination of the religious. Cf. canon 1425, § 2. If a parish has been merely entrusted to a religious community temporarily, the commitment may be made in virtue of a faculty possessed by the Apostolic Delegate. Cf. *Index Facultatum Quas Pro Locis Missionis Suae, Nuntiis, Internuntiis et Delegatis Apostolicis Penes Civitates Seu Nationes, Post Codicis Iuris Canonici Publicationem Tribuere SSmus Dominus Noster Decrevit, Ceteris Abrogatis,* n. 48, apud Vermeersch-Creusen, *Epitome* (5. ed., 3 vols., Mechliniae-Romae: Dessain, 1933), I, 639.

have been offered by canonists in order to effect a reconcilation of the apparently contradictory laws of canons 630, § 4, and 1182, § 1. A certain writer [94] mentions a given opinion, although he cites no defenders of it. According to this possible opinion, which Nebreda himself does not hold, the local ordinary has true administrative power and the religious pastor has the same power. The acceptance of such a view would not involve a contradiction of the two laws, because it would parallel the relationship which exists between the pope and all other administrators of ecclesiastical property. For the pope and the lawfully constituted administrator of any parcel of ecclesiastical property have power over the same unit, and in each case it is ordinary power. Hence, if the pope does not act directly concerning the administration of the property, the subordinate administrator has ordinary and immediate administrative rights over it and requires no delegation in order to perform validly his duties. Of course the subordinate administrator would have to yield if the pope decided to exercise immediate administrative power. This opinion does not seem correct because canon 1182, § 1, apparently makes provision for the fact that there may be an exception to the general rule of a rector administering the property of the church. This exception seems to be contained in the words *"nisi aliud ex speciali titulo vel legitima consuetudine constet."*

The second opinion, espoused by Nebreda himself,[95] declares that in such a conflict of rights we must presume the existence of a solution which does not weaken the power of one party at the expense of the other. In this opinion the local ordinary has not immediate administrative power, but only the power of supervision over the immediate administration which belongs exclusively to the pastor. However, this opinion also seems to pay no regard to the phrase *"nisi aliud ex speciali titulo vel legitima consuetudine constet."*

The third opinion holds that the right to administer immediately

[94] Cf. Nebreda, "De loci Ordinariorum iuribus circa pia legata donationesve tum Religiosis tum eorum ecclesiis etiam paroecialibus facta," *CpR*, VII (1926), 197.

[95] *Ibid.*, p. 197.

the churches which are secular belongs to the local ordinary, who may delegate this power to the pastor.[96] Blat[97] states that the phrase *"nisi aliud ex speciali titulo . . . constet"* points to other canons in the general law. This seems to be the key to the solution of the difficulty and involves no straining of terms which seems practically to be inherent in the second opinion concerning this question. Certainly, the local ordinary's administration should cause no practical inconvenience in the way of diminished returns to the religious community, for the powers granted to the local ordinary by canon 630, § 4, are restricted definitely to the functions named in that canon, that is, to the administrative acts which are concerned with the construction, the upkeep, the rebuilding and the decoration of the church. The religious pastor at such a church would therefore retain the right of administration which deals with the acceptance of a salary and emoluments attached to the office of pastor. It is true that, if the local ordinary exercised his immediate administrative rights, the pastor would have little to say about the acts mentioned in canon 630, § 4, and his ideas as to the church edifice would be of no avail in a building or repair plan. However, even if he had immediate administrative powers, he would still be subject to the supervision and the decrees of the local ordinary. This is especially true at the present time when some dioceses have established "building commissions" to supervise the construction and the repair of churches.[98] In fact, in the great generality of cases the local ordinary will permit the pastor to administer the property of the church as well as that of the parish. Of course the ordinary will in any event retain the right of supervision according to the norm of canon 1519.

The administrative rights of the local ordinary over churches

[96] Vermeersch-Creusen, *Epitome,* I, 478; Bouuaert-Simenon, *Manuale Iuris Canonici* (3. ed., Gandae et Leodii: 1930), I, 410; Blat, *Commentarium,* I, 702; Coronata, *Institutiones Iuris Canonici,* I, 825.

[97] *Commentarium* lib. III, pars II-VI, 39.

[98] *Acta et Decreta Concilii Provincialis Portlandensis in Oregon Quarti,* Decreta 333-337.

which are considered to be *religious* churches [99] present a more difficult problem. If the church is a religious church, that is, if it is one which is either owned by the community or in the perpetual or quasi-perpetual use of the religious community, then the religious superior has the right to administer immediately all the property which is destined for the construction, the repair, the conservation and the decoration of the church.[100] This power extends to churches which are not owned, but which are merely entrusted perpetually or quasi-perpetually to religious communities. This conclusion, apart from the extrinsic authority of several commentators,[101] has a basis in the words of canon 609, § 1, which states that the norm of canon 415 is to be applied to parochial churches "at which a religious community resides." Now, canon 415 declares that in the event of such a union the moral person is to administer the property of the church as well as the pious legacies which may come to the church. Therefore, the right to administer immediately the property of the church seems to belong to the religious community, even when the church is not in the dominion of the community.

The chief difficulty concerning the administration of the churches of religious communities concerns the supervisory rights of the local ordinary over such administration. Vromant [102] states that even exempt religious superiors must give an account of their administration of the property of religious parochial churches to the local ordinary. In support of his opinion he appeals to a decision of the Pontifical Commission for the Interpretation of the canons of the

[99] Cf. p. 86 for the definition of a *religious* church.

[100] Cf. canon 630, § 4. "Non obstante voto paupertatis, eidem Religioso, qui paroeciam regit sive titulo parochi sive titulo vicarii licet eleemosynas in bonum paroecianorum, vel pro scholis catholicis aut locis piis paroeciae coniunctis, quovis modo oblatas accipere aut colligere, et acceptas sive collectas administrare, itemque, servata offerentium voluntate, pro prudenti suo arbitrio, erogare, salva semper vigilantia sui Superioris; *sed eleemosynas pro ecclesia paroeciali aedificanda, conservanda, instauranda, exornanda accipere, apud se retinere, colligere aut administrare pertinet ad Superiores, si ecclesia sit communitatis religiosae; secus ad loci Ordinarium.*"

[101] Cf. p. 86.

[102] *De Bonis Ecclesiae Temporalibus*, p. 217.

Code.[103] Cocchi [104] and Vermeersch-Creusen [105] hold the same opinion as Vromant. However, as is evident, this response refers to religious parishes and not to religious churches; and therefore, since canon 630, § 4, deals precisely with the right of the religious superior over the administration of religious *churches,* the response gives no satisfactory answer to the difficulty concerning the local ordinary's right to supervise the administration performed by the religious superiors with regard to the property of religious churches.

On the other hand Maroto [106] declares that the religious superiors, even though they belong to a non-exempt religious institute, have no obligation to render to the local ordinary an account of the administration of the property of the religious church. He argues that this opinion is clearly contained in canon 630, § 4, which makes no distinction based upon religious exemption. Melo [107] holds that regular superiors who invest such money in order to obtain interest do not require the consent or the supervision of the local ordinary. He also appeals to canon 630, § 4. Coronata practically agrees with Melo and says that any money which has been given to the churches of regulars is not subject to the supervision of the local ordinary.[108] Nebreda denies that the local ordinary has any supervision over the property of religious churches and cites canon 618, § 2, 1°, in support of his opinion.[109] Mayer holds the same opinion,[110] but restricts its application to those churches which are owned by the religious community. Although he also accepts the opinion that a

[103] "An vi canonum 631, § 1; 535, § 3, 2°; 533, § 1, 3°-4°, *loci Ordinarius ius habet exigendi rationes administrationis fundorum legatorumve paroeciae religiosae,* de qua in canone 1425, § 2?

R. Affirmative, *firmis praescriptis canonum* 630, § 4; 1550. 25 iulii 1926, ad IV—*AAS,* XVIII (1926), 393.

[104] *Commentarium,* Lib. III, Pars VI, 394.

[105] *Epitome,* II, 303.

[106] "Annotationes," *CpR,* VII (1926), 440.

[107] *De Exemptione Regularium,* The Catholic University of America, Canon Law Studies, n. 12 (Washington: The Catholic University of America, 1921), p. 90.

[108] *Institutiones Iuris Canonici,* I, 825.

[109] Cf. "De loci Ordinariorum iuribus circa pia legata donationesve tum Religiosis tum eorum ecclesiis etiam paroecialibus facta"—*CpR,* VII (1926), 195.

[110] "Die nicht inkorporierte Klosterpfarrei"—*AKKR,* CXII (1932), p. 479.

religious church is one which is either in the dominion or in the perpetual or quasi-perpetual use of a religious community, he thinks that only the ownership and not the use of the church entitles the religious superiors to exemption in this matter from the local ordinary. This opinion seems to be the best of any advanced, because it is hard to agree that the mere use of a church, even perpetually given, should exclude all supervisory power of the superior of the moral person who retains the right of dominion.

In the matter of the portion of the parish income which is due to the church edifice as such, Mayer [111] in his detailed treatment of this subject declares that, if the parish which uses the church must contribute to the support of the edifice from the *endowment of the parish,* the latter is administered by the pastor with the obligation of giving a determined share of the income from the endowment to the religious superior for the upkeep of the church. This determined share of the income would be based upon an agreement between the religious superiors and the local ordinary, since the latter would have the right to supervise a parochial endowment. If there is no permanent church fund and the church subsists on the alms of the people, even if these offer only a partial support for the edifice, then the religious superior has the right to collect, retain and administer the alms given for the erection, conservation, repair or ornamentation of the church.

When, as it frequently happens, the collection in the church is taken up and used for both the parish and the church, then the religious superiors and the local ordinary should have some previous agreement by which there is a clear understanding about the percentage of the collection which is to be used for each purpose. In this way the complaints of the parishioners will be forestalled. Otherwise they may feel that too much of the collection money has been used for the support of the church to the detriment of other parish buildings.

In the case where the church is a religious church in the sense that it is not owned by the religious house or institute, but has been given to it with the right of perpetual or quasi-perpetual use, the permission of the local ordinary is required before the administrator

[111] *Ibidem.*

of the church may undertake any extraordinary repairs or rebuilding. This permission does not take from the religious superior the right to administer the work of repair or rebuilding. However, the right of the local ordinary to supervise the administration of the money which belongs to such a parochial church cannot be denied.[112]

Since in the case here under consideration the church is not only a religious church but at the same time a parochial church, an apparent conflict of rights may arise between the pastor and the religious superior. This may happen when the collections for the church appear to be excessive and by the same token occasion a less generous support for the other parochial necessities. In such case, since the church is parochial, the local ordinary will have a great interest in the controversy and may support the pastor who rightfully claims that the collections for the church are excessive. In case of such a conflict the religious superior would have to yield to the decree of the local ordinary. The religious superior could have recourse to the Holy See.[113]

Despite the fact that the reasons here advanced for the maintained opinion concerning the right of the local ordinary to supervise the administration of *religious* parochial churches appear to furnish greater probability than do the reasons which underlie the contrary opinion, there is not excluded the possibility that an authentic interpretation of canon 630, § 4, may declare that the local ordinary has the right to supervise the administration of *religious* parochial churches regardless of the source of the income which is used for the administrative work.

(IV) *Property of the cathedral church.* The local ordinary is the co-administrator with the cathedral chapter of the cathedral church and its possessions. This right is enunciated in canon 1182,

[112] Vromant, "De donis quae missionariis sive saecularibus sive religiosis quandoque ab extraneis mittuntur," *Periodica,* XVIII (1929), pp. 22*-23*.

[113] This seems to follow from canon 631, § 2, which speaks directly of the work of the pastor. By implication it appears that the religious superior would have to yield to the local ordinary in any dispute which concerns collections taken up in the church for the benefit of the church. Canons 1171, 609, § 3, and 482 also show that the local ordinary has the right to judge whether there is any infringement on parochial rights in other matters which are handled by religious and possibly with damage to parochial rights.

§ 1.[114] Although Vromant [115] declares that the ordinary has the right merely to supervise the administration of the property of the cathedral church if the latter is at the same time a parochial church, this seems to be a too literal interpretation of the words of canon 415, § 3, 3°, which attribute to the chapter the right to administer the property of a cathedral church which is at the same time a parochial church.[116] For canon 1182, § 1, seems to be a more detailed application of the law of canon 415, which application makes no exception to the immediate right of the local ordinary to administer the property of the cathedral church. Rather, canon 415, as is clear from its introductory words, determines the division of duties between the pastor and the Chapter, and applies to collegiate as well as to cathedral churches.[117] There appears no sound reason why the Code should restrict the right of the local ordinary, especially over his own cathedral church. Therefore, it seems correct to maintain, despite the lack of explicit treatment of this subject by post-Code authors, that, even when the cathedral church is also a parochial church, the local ordinary continues to be the co-administrator of the property of the church. Co-administration here means that both the bishop and the chapter need the consent of each other before either can validly determine anything concerning the administration of the church or of its property.[118]

In dioceses or territories which have no cathedral chapters the co-administration of the cathedral church does not pass to the *coetus consultorum*, which must be constituted by the ordinary in place of the chapter. Such a right is not given by the Code, which states in canon 427 that this group is to assist in the government of the diocese.[119] Blat [120] and Vromant [121] cite canon 427 as a confirmation

[114] The text of the canon is given on p. 86.

[115] *De Bonis Ecclesiae Temporalibus*, p. 215.

[116] "§ 3. Ad Capitulum spectat:

"3° Ecclesiae curam habere eiusque bona administrare cum piis legatis."

[117] "§ 1. Si ecclesia cathedralis aut collegialis simul sit paroecialis, relationes inter Capitulum et parochum reguntur normis quae sequuntur, . . ."

[118] S. R. R., *Causa Corduben. in America*, 1 feb. 1915—*AAS*, VII (1915), 131-133. The Rota in this case declared that the bishop and the chapter had equal power in administering the property of the church.

[119] "Coetus consultorum dioecesanorum vices Capituli cathedralis, qua

of their opinion that the *coetus consultorum* has the right to co-administer the property of the cathedral church. However, the very wording of the canon seems to restrict the right of this group to the administration of the property of the diocese considered as a moral person apart from the church which has been designated as the cathedral church.

In mission territories the *consilium missionariorum*, which the ordinary must establish according to the norm of canon 302, does not hold the place of the cathedral chapter. The ordinary of the territory must consult these counsellors in the more important and difficult affairs which affect the whole territory. Although he is not obliged to do so, it very often happens that the ordinary will associate with himself some others who will assist him in the administration of the quasi-cathedral church.[122] Just as the law attributes equality of rights and duties to a pastor and a quasi-pastor,[123] so too it states that the quasi-pastor of a quasi-parish has the right to administer the offerings made for the benefit of his territorial division in a mission field. The term "missio," as used in canon 1182, § 2, refers to a quasi-parish which is defined in canon 216, § 1, 3°, as the territorial division of a vicariate or prefecture apostolic which has been assigned to a special rector. Therefore, in accordance with the norm of canon 1182, § 2, which states that the pastor has the right to administer the property of the parish or mission, the pastor of a çathedral quasi-parish in mission territory has the same right as the pastor of a cathedral parish in any other territory.[124]

Episcopi senatus, supplet; quare quae canones ad gubernationem dioecesis, sive sede plena sive ea impedita aut vacante, Capitulo cathedrali tribuunt, ea de coetu quoque consultorum dioecesanorum intelligenda sunt." Cf. also Vermeersch-Creusen, *Epitome,* II, 302; Augustine, *A Commentary,* VI, 52-53; Coronata, *Institutiones Iuris Canonici,* II, 57; Ayrinhac, *Administrative Legislation in the Code of Canon Law,* p. 33.

[120] *Commentarium,* lib. III, pars II-VI, 39.

[121] *De Bonis Ecclesiae Temporalibus,* p. 214.

[122] S. C. de Prop. Fide, epist. (ad Episcopos, Vicarios Praefectosque Apostolicos ac Missionum Superiores.), die Paschae Resurrectionis, 1922, nn. 13 et 85—*AAS,* XIV (1922), 290, 300; Vromant, *De Bonis Ecclesiae Temporalibus,* pp. 214-215.

[123] Canon 451, § 2, 1°.

[124] In so much as there is no explicit provision in the Code concerning the

(V) *Alms which have been donated for a charitable purpose which is unspecified.* The local ordinary exclusively may dispose of alms which have been left in a general way for charitable purposes but without any specific designation of the beneficiary.[125]

(VI) *The bequests contained in wills.* According to canon 1517, §§ 1-2, the local ordinary may at times reduce the burdens imposed by the wills of those who have died. This right of the ordinary may be exercised when it is clear that the deceased has made such provision in the will as cannot be carried out, or when the duties imposed by the testator have become impossible of fulfillment. The right to diminish the obligations of the beneficiaries does not, however, comprise the right to effect a reduction in the number of Masses to be said, for in this matter the Holy See functions with exclusive right, unless the testator has expressly permitted the ordinary the use of this right.[126] It is to be noted that the local ordinary has the right to designate the recipients of the charitable bequest if the testator has not expressly designated them.[127] However, if the bequest is left simply to an exempt religious community for purposes purely internal in that institute, then the major superior is the ordinary who has the power to execute the designated distribution of the bequest.[128]

administration of the property of a cathedral quasi-parish, it seems that the parallel norm of canon 415, § 2, 5°, must be followed. Moreover, the norm of canon 1182, § 2, covers this case, unless there should be special legislation for a cathedral quasi-parish. There is no evidence of such special legislation.

[125] Vromant, *De Bonis Ecclesiae Temporalibus,* p. 204. This author also claims that this right of the local ordinary may be extended to the income from the property left to a church provided that the income has not been designated specifically for any special use. However, this seems to be an unwarranted extension, because the general principle, "Accessorium sequitur suum principale," demands that the income from the principal must be devoted to the same cause as the principal itself, unless the donor has made a specific intention with regard to the income from the principal.

[126] Pont. Comm. Intr., 14 iulii 1922, ad XI—*AAS,* XIV (1922), 529.

[127] Hannan, *The Canon Law of Wills,* The Catholic University of America, Canon Law Studies (Washington: The Catholic University of America, 1934), p. 455.

[128] Canon 1515, § 1, includes religious ordinaries as well as local ordinaries.

(VII) *The revenue accruing from the establishment of pensions and the levying of taxes.*

(a) *Pensions.* A pension is the right granted to someone by a competent ecclesiastical superior for a just cause to receive some part of the annual income of another's benefice.[129] According to canon 1429, §§ 1-2, the local ordinary may establish pensions on benefices or parishes, but always within certain restrictions. He can place a pension on a benefice in the very act of conferring the benefice, provided there is a just cause and the pension will not last longer than the life of the beneficiary, who also must be assured of a decent support before the pension may be established. Who may be given such pensions? The local ordinary may establish a pension on a parish provided that the pension is granted in favor of a retiring or departing pastor or vicar and that it does not exceed one-third of the certain revenues of the parish, after deducting all necessary expenses from the *certain* revenues.

In each case the beneficiary or the pastor must be assured of a decent income to support him in a position becoming his dignity. The amount should be a definite sum, even though the necessary expenses may vary to some extent from time to time.[130]

Among the certain income which forms the basis for determining the pension are the returns from immovable property, interest on invested money and any assured income from other sources. Stole fees and free will offerings are by no means certain and are not to be computed in reckoning the pension.[131] There is no justification for a tax which is necessary only in order to pay a pension which cannot be paid from the ordinary assured income.[132] It is worthy of note that there may be more than one who receives the benefit of the pension, provided that the total amount of the pension does not exceed one-third of the assured revenues; for example, a retiring

[129] Wernz, *Ius Decretalium,* II, n. 321.

[130] Vromant, *De Bonis Ecclesiae Temporalibus,* p. 125.

[131] E. Suarez, "De Pensionibus, beneficiis paroecialibus imponendis," *Angelicum,* VI (1929), 225-226; Vromant, *op. cit.,* p. 124; Blat, *Commentarium,* lib. III, pars II-VI, p. 409.

[132] Augustine, *The Canonical and Civil Status of Catholic Parishes in the United States* (St. Louis: Herder, 1926), p. 218. Cf. canons 1505, 1506.

pastor and a sick curate may each be in need of the support afforded by the pension.[133] Also worthy of note is the fact that a pension may be paid to a pastor who is asked to resign in order to prevent his removal; such a pension would not be considered simony.[134] Since the law does not require the observance of any special solemnities in the establishment of a pension, it seems that such an act is not alienation in the canonical sense. This application differs from that of the old law which considered such acts as equivalent to alienation and, therefore, beyond the power of the ordinary.[135]

The establishment of a pension on quasi-parishes in mission territory or even on mission stations which have not been erected into quasi-parishes must be in accord with certain rules which apply especially to mission lands. Such pensions demand that the priest who is to receive the pension has been stationed for ten years in the quasi-parish or mission station, that his resignation is due to sickness and that the basis of the pension should be the total income, less expenses, which the quasi-parish or mission station receives during the year.[136] Therefore stole fees, if particular law grants these to the quasi-parish, and free-will offerings are to be reckoned among other income as the basis for determining the proportionate amount of the pension. Moreover, the expenses to be deducted are not so extensive as those mentioned in canon 1429, § 2, for parochial benefices. The law of canon 1429, § 2, allows deduction of all necessary expenses, whereas the mission law does not add the word "quibusvis" and seems to refer only to those expenses which are necessary merely for the upkeep of the church, for the performance of the sacred functions and for the gathering of income. Apparently the mission law does not allow for a previous deduction of the quasi-pastor's salary before computing the amount of the pension. Of course, the amount

133 Suarez, *art. cit.*, pp. 224-225.

134 S. C. C., *Dioecesis N.*, 11 nov. 1922—*AAS*, XV (1923), 454-456; Pont. Comm. Intr., 20 maii 1923, ad IX—*AAS*, XVI (1923), 116.

135 Suarez, *art. cit.*, p. 225.

136 Formulae Facultatum quas S. C. de Prop. Fide Ordinariis in terris missionum procurat: Formula tertia major, n. XLV,—Vermeersch-Creusen, *Epitome*, I, 533.

of the pension cannot be so large that it will deprive the quasi-pastor of the "*portio congrua*" to which he is entitled.[137]

(b) *The levying of taxes.*

(1) *The seminary tax.* The amount of this tax will depend upon the needs of the seminary. However, it must not exceed five per cent of the income of the moral person which is taxed. The persons subject to the tax as well as the basis for reckoning the tax are declared in canon 1356.

(2) *The cathedraticum.* This tax must be a moderate sum which is intended not as a means of episcopal support but as a sign of subjection to episcopal authority.[138] The amount of the tax is to be determined by a provincial council or by a conference of the bishops in a province. The stated sum must be approved by the Holy See. Custom may also determine the tax, provided that the custom is of long standing, namely, at least a custom of forty years duration.[139]

(3) *Exactions imposed upon an ecclesiastical moral person at the time of its foundation or constitution as a moral person.* The levy of such a tax requires as a cause the common good of the diocese or the great need of the person who is the patron of the church or moral person.[140] It is to be noted that when the moral person has received its juridical status, or if the moral person be a church, its consecration, and no tax has been levied upon it at that time, then the ordinary cannot later impose a tax upon it, excepting the cathedraticum and the taxes mentioned in canon 1505.[141]

In addition to the seminary tax and the establishment of a pension which is to be derived from the benefice canon 1505 permits the local ordinary to impose upon the beneficiaries moderate taxes in extraordinary cases when the special needs of the diocese require

[137] Vromant, *De Bonis Ecclesiae Temporalibus*, pp. 126-127.

[138] Canon 1504; S. C. C., *Dioecesis N. in Gallia*, 13 martii 1920—*AAS*, XII (1920), 446-447; cf. Doheny, *Church Property: Modes of Acquisition*, p. 56.

[139] Pistocchi, *De Bonis Ecclesiae Temporalibus*, p. 125; Coronata, *Institutiones Iuris Canonici*, II, 447.

[140] Canon 1506.

[141] Cf. Ayrinhac, *Administrative Legislation in the New Code of Canon Law*, p. 400.

such taxes.[142] The law does not determine the amount of the tax; it merely declares that it should be moderate. It is to be noted that such a tax is an extraordinary means and not the ordinary or usual means of supporting the diocese.[143]

(VIII) *The property of divided or extinct parishes.* The local ordinary in virtue of canon 1427, § 1, has the power under certain conditions to divide parishes and benefices in such a way that there is a reallocation of territory and a redistribution of property title.[144] In order to exercise this power there should be present a canonical reason for such action. According to canon 1427, § 2, this cause is present if the people of the parish have to undergo great inconvenience in order to attend the parochial church, or if the number of parishioners is so large that the present parish cannot meet their spiritual needs. However, according to canon 1422 only the Holy See can suppress a benefice, and this right includes parishes, even those in the United States. The parishes of the United States are true benefices, as is clear from a letter addressed to the Apostolic Delegate.[145] The law of canon 1422 concerning the exclusive right of the Holy See to suppress a benefice is not in conflict with the law of canon 2292 which declares that the local ordinary with the advice of his council has the right to suppress in a penal manner the parochial seat of residence. For as Vromant well says,[146] canon 2292 does not refer to the suppression of the parish but of the parochial seat of residence, for example, by the assignment of the care of the parish to a neighboring pastor.

Vromant thinks, but without sufficient reason, that the local ordinary can suppress a benefice which at the time of its erection had no dowry.[147] His opinion seems to invoke a distinction unwarranted

[142] "Loci Ordinarius, praeter tributum pro Seminario, de quo in can. 1355, 1356, aut beneficialem pensionem de qua in can. 1429, potest, speciali dioecesis necessitate impellente, omnibus beneficiariis, sive saecularibus sive religiosis, extraordinariam et moderatam exactionem imponere."

[143] Doheny, *Church Property: Modes of Acquisition,* p. 59.

[144] Cf. S. C. C., *Utinen.,* 14 ianuarii 1922—*AAS,* XIV (1922), 229-231.

[145] Cf. Bouscaren, *Canon Law Digest,* I, pp. 150-151.

[146] *De Bonis Ecclesiae Temporalibus,* p. 83.

[147] *De Bonis Ecclesiae Temporalibus,* p. 84.

by canon 1422, since the latter speaks in general and unqualified terms when it refers to the suppression of benefices.

In addition to its suppression by a legitimate superior, a benefice may also lose its juridical personality through its failure to exist as such for a hundred years.[148]

In his act of dividing a parochial benefice the legitimate superior is entitled also to divide the property of the benefice. In order to be fair to each party which is affected by the division, the general debts of the benefice, that is, those which have been contracted for the entire territory, must also be divided in proportion to the ability of each new moral person to meet those debts.[149] As is stated in canon 1500, the legitimate superior in his act of dividing the territory and the common property has no right to dispose of property which already has been designated by the donors for special purposes. If the property of the original benefice has already been designated for a certain purpose by the statutes which were enacted in connection with the erection of the original benefice, or if its allotment has been restricted by the acquired rights of a third party, then it cannot be divided for the general use of the new moral persons arising out of the division.[150]

In the event that a benefice or a parish or any moral person is suppressed the moral ecclesiastical person immediately superior in rank becomes the owner of the remaining property. The intentions of the original donors, the previously acquired rights and the special statutes by which the suppressed moral person formerly was governed must of course be respected and observed in the distribution and absorption of the property.[151] Therefore, the property of a suppressed parish will pass to the ownership of the diocese. The same holds true for the property of a non-collegiate moral person, for the diocese is the immediately superior moral person.[152] The

[148] Canon 102, § 1.

[149] Ayrinhac, *Administrative Legislation in the New Code of Canon Law*, pp. 387-388; Vermeersch-Creusen, *Epitome*, II, 507. Cf. canon 1500.

[150] Ayrinhac, *Administrative Legislation in the New Code of Canon Law*, pp. 387-388; Vromant, *De Bonis Ecclesiae Temporalibus*, p. 79.

[151] Canon 1501.

[152] Vromant, *De Bonis Ecclesiae Temporalibus*, p. 85; Coronata, *Institutiones Iuris Canonici*, II, 443.

more common and acceptable opinion concerning the transfer of property in the suppression of an association of the laity constituted as a moral person is that the property passes to the diocese, unless the association is immediately subject to the Holy See.[153] In the case in which a moral person has not yet been suppressed but at the same time is not functioning as such, then during the hundred years required for the extinction of its status of moral personality, the moral person immediately superior to it has the right to administer the property.[154]

(IX) *Property which the ordinary administers in virtue of a special title of administration.* Finally, although the local ordinary does not by reason of his office have the right to administer some particular unit of ecclesiastical property which is within his territory, he may acquire the right to do so in virtue of a legal prescription which fulfills all the conditions mentioned in canons 1508-1512. Although Vromant seems to think that the words of canon 1519, § 1, "salvis legitimis praescriptionibus, etc.," refer only to prescription as used in canons 1508-1512,[155] this phrase has a wider application and may include any enactment which has the force of law, for example, a privilege or a concordat, or the documents of foundation.[156]

It should be noted that, apart from the immediate administrative rights listed in the preceding pages, the local ordinary's administrative power is restricted to that of supervision. He may not transfer the property of one parish to another parish. This is clear from the fact that canon 1519 does not give to the local ordinary the distributive power which canon 1518 asserts as inherent in the papacy. However, the most forceful argument against the local ordinary's possession of such power is to be found in canon 1422. This canon states that the Holy See alone has the right to dismember a benefice in the sense that its property is appropriated without the erection

[153] Vermeersch-Creusen, *Epitome,* II, 507; Vromant, *op. cit.,* p. 85; Coronata, *op. cit.,* II, 444.

[154] Vermeersch-Creusen, *Epitome,* II, 507.

[155] *De Bonis Ecclesiae Temporalibus,* pp. 205-206.

[156] Cf. Blat, *Commentarium,* lib. III, pars II-VI, pp. 528-529; Pistocchi, *De Bonis Ecclesiae Temporalibus,* pp. 312-313; Coronata, *Institutiones Iuris Canonici,* II, 473; Ayrinhac, *Administrative Legislation in the New Code of Canon Law,* p. 425.

of a new benefice.[157] As is clear from a decision of the Sacred Congregation of the Council,[158] the basic reason for the reservation of such acts to the Holy See is the fact that the act of dismemberment, which normally entails a change in property title, is strictly a donation, namely, an alienation without corresponding compensation. Such a donation very frequently is contrary to the will of the original donor, and the ordinary has not the power which suffices to supplant the donor's requisite consent. Inasmuch, then, as any act of dismemberment, as here understood, entails not simply the usual form of alienation but also the form of outright donation, the ordinary lacks all competence to authorize or permit it, regardless of the amount of value involved in such a transaction.[159]

Article 4. The Formal Extension of the Local Ordinary's Supervisory Power

The supervisory power which canon 1519, § 1, attributes to the local ordinary in relation to non-exempt ecclesiastical property within his territory is explained more in detail in the next paragraph of this canon and in the succeeding canons. The second paragraph of canon 1519 empowers the local ordinary to issue special instructions which do not infringe upon the rights of subordinate administrators, in

[157] "Unio exstinctiva beneficiorum, eorum suppressio, aut *dismembratio quae detractis bonis beneficialibus fiat quin novum erigatur beneficium*; unio aeque aut minus principalis beneficii religiosi cum saeculari et contra, itemque beneficii religiosi translatio, divisio et dismembratio quaelibet *uni Sedi Apostolicae reservantur.*"

[158] S. C. C., *Utinen.*, 14 ianuarii 1922—*AAS*, XIV (1922), 231-232.

[159] "Contra, canone 1422 reservatur Apostolicae Sedi tantum *dismembratio bonorum beneficii* seu paroeciae, nempe 'quae detractis bonis beneficialibus fiat quin novum erigatur beneficium.' Ratio huius reservationis Apostolicae non videtur, hodie, proprie in eo consistere quod in casu agatur de vera alienatione bonorum ecclesiasticorum; quia secus eam Ordinarii, saltem ad tramitem iuris Codicis, vi canonis 1532, usque ad summum lib. 30,000 peragere valerent. Ex adverso, id repetendum videtur—praeterquam ad praecavendos abusus inde forsan orituros, ne scilicet ut unum adornetur altare expolietur alterum—ex eo quod in themate agitur de alienatione *absque compensatione seu pretio,* idest de vera bonorum ecclesiasticorum *donatione,* cui saepius obstat contraria fundatorum vel oblatorum voluntas, ad quam supplendam minime protenditur Ordinariorum potestas."—*Op. et loc. cit.*

order that these administrators may perform their duties concerning the temporal possessions entrusted to their care. The instructions issued for their guidance must be opportune and circumspect, that is, balanced by a consideration of attendant circumstances, of extant legitimate customs and of prior rights.

The canon states that legitimate customs and previously acquired rights must be respected by the ordinary who issues the instructions. According to canon 4 all rights acquired through the earlier law retain their force even after the promulgation of the Code law, unless they have been expressly revoked by the canons in the Code. Decrees issued by the local ordinary against such rights are invalid, unless the Holy See has given such abolitional power to the local ordinary.[160] The rights mentioned in canon 1519, § 2, include those which have their source in concordats, legitimate prescriptions and privileges.[161]

Before issuing instructions the local ordinary must also take into consideration the legitimate customs which make certain norms inadvisable. He should bear in mind that a custom *secundum legem* is the best interpreter of the law. Of course, he has the right and competence to investigate whether the customary practice is really *secundum legem.* If the custom is contrary to or above the diocesan law (*contra legem vel praeter legem*), then the local ordinary may legislate with due regard to the norm of canon 30.[162] Therefore, a law as to the administration of property which affects the whole diocese does not revoke the contrary custom in a particular parish, since it is probable that a parish can establish a custom;[163] nor does a special law of the ordinary revoke a contrary centenary or imme-

160 Pistocchi, *De Bonis Ecclesiae Temporalibus,* p. 313.

161 Coronata, *Institutiones Iuris Canonici,* II, 473; Pistocchi, *De Bonis Ecclesiae Temporalibus,* p. 313. Cf. also canons 3, 1508-1512, 63-79, for fuller details on these rights.

162 "Firmo praescripto can. 5, consuetudo contra legem vel praeter legem per contrariam consuetudinem aut legem revocatur; sed, nisi expressam de iisdem mentionem fecerit, lex non revocat consuetudines centenarias aut immemorabiles, nec lex generalis consuetudines particulares."

163 Guilfoyle, *Custom,* The Catholic University of America, Canon Law Studies, n. 105 (Washington: The Catholic University of America, 1937), pp. 95-96.

morial custom unless the law expressly singles out such a custom for revocation. However, the continued right to employ a contrary custom presupposes of necessity that the custom has effectively acquired the force of law, namely, that it has the competent superior's consent, that it has been the practice of a community which is capable of receiving a law, and that it is vested with the continuous and complete duration of time demanded by the law of the Code. Code law requires a duration of forty years before any existing law can be supplanted by contrary custom, and duration of one hundred years or a period of time immemorial for the supplanting of any law which in addition prohibits the formation of a contrary custom.[164] A custom which is reprobated by law, and therefore may never be invoked against any law, can likewise not prevail against any decrees of the ordinary in as much as it must be considered an unreasonable practice from its very inception.[165] Therefore, for example, no one can appeal to custom in defense of the practice of *demanding* at the church door contributions from the faithful who are entering the church at the time of divine services. Even a collection for a seat in the church at such divine services is prohibited.[166]

Circumstances which are peculiar to the territory, even if they be only temporary, also have a bearing on the instructions of the ordinary to subordinate administrators. Thus, serious labor troubles or extremely high prices in the building trades may be the reason why an ordinary prohibits for a time any building project which is not immediately necessary; high commodity costs within the territory

[164] Cf. canons 25-27; also Cicognani, *Canon Law*, p. 663.

[165] Canon 27, § 2.

[166] Cf. canon 1181. Cf. also the statement made by the Sacred Congregation of the Propagation of the Faith and addressed to the bishops of the United States in 1869: "Praxim pecunias exigendi ad fores ecclesiarum ut fideles ingredi possint, et divinis mysteriis adesse . . . penitus aboleri atque eliminari cupiens, S. Congregatio A. Tuam nunc in Domino adhortari non desinit, ut omnem curam conferas, si forte in aliquibus istius dioecesis locis consuetudinem huiusmodi invaluisse noveris, *ne ulli omnino collectores,* quando christifideles in ecclesiam ingrediantur, quo divinis mysteriis adstare, vel verbum Dei audire possint, ad earundem ecclesiarum fores ponantur." *American Ecclesiastical Review,* XLV (1911), 595-596. This statement is there mentioned by the Apostolic Delegate who calls special attention to the words "ne ulli omnino collectores . . . ad ecclesiarum fores ponantur."

may influence the ordinary to command that a certain minimum wage be paid to the employees of church administrators. In general, circumstances must be considered in order to make the instructions suitable to time and place.

After a consideration of the various rights, customs and circumstances which affect the administration of church property, the local ordinary is empowered to issue "instructions" which will enable the inferior administrators to perform their duties more easily and efficiently. An "instruction" is a document which has for its purpose greater clarification of existing laws in order that the laws may become more effective.[167] Generally an instruction does not have the force of a law, but rather has a directive force which seeks to facilitate or insist upon the observance of already existing laws. However, it obliges a subject to obedience, since it is a part of the necessary ecclesiastical discipline.[168]

Canon 1519, § 2, at first sight seems to allow the ordinary only the right to expedite the temporal administration by instructions which embody definite plans for more efficient management. However, in virtue of canon 335, § 1, which declares that the local ordinary has legislative power in temporal matters as well as in spiritual affairs, it seems that the bishop has more than a merely directive power; he has the right to make laws which oblige inferior administrators who are subject to him. However, as was mentioned above, these laws must reflect due consideration for acquired rights and legitimate customs.

The instructions issued by the local ordinary must not exceed the limits of the common law. Therefore, the decrees cannot validly restrict any administrative rights which the common law of the Church has specifically granted to other administrators. This restric-

[167] Benedictus XV, motu prop., *Cum iuris canonici,* 15 sept. 1917—*AAS,* IX (1917), 484. Although the definition of the Pope was given specifically with regard to instructions from the Sacred Congregations, it seems that the nature of an instruction is the same for all cases, even for episcopal instructions. Coronata (*Institutiones Iuris Canonici,* I, 16) and Maroto (*Institutiones Iuris Canonici,* I, n. 180) define instruction in this way and do not restrict their definition to papal instructions or to instructions from the Holy See. Cf. also Pistocchi, *De Bonis Ecclesiae Temporalibus,* p. 315.

[168] Cf. Maroto, *op. et loc. cit.*; Coronata, *op. et loc. cit.*

tion also applies not only to his instructions but also to his legislative power in the strict sense.[169] Therefore, the local ordinary cannot validly recall to himself the administration of all ecclesiastical property within his territory.[170] The instructions of the ordinary cannot command anything which is clearly forbidden by the general law, although they may deal with matters which are not clearly expressed in the law or which are *praeter legem*.[171] If it is doubtful that the ordinary has exceeded his powers in this matter the inferior administrator must obey, since in a doubt of this kind the superior must be obeyed.[172] Nevertheless, although the subject must obey, he may have recourse to the Holy See, and if the ordinary has removed him from the parish or benefice, the appointment to such a parish or benefice cannot be given perpetually to another until the Holy See has sustained the decree of the ordinary.[173]

The purpose of the instruction is to insure that the entire work of temporal administration will be managed satisfactorily. Therefore, the instruction must be timely, that is, it must fit the specific needs of the special occasion that evokes it. The reasons for such a timely intervention may be occasioned by the cognizance which must be taken of the various interrelated details of the financial report, or also by the direct request of a beneficiary or of a pastor who is seeking an acceptable solution for certain specific administrative problems. At any rate, instructions will have little good effect unless they have a worthwhile object. As Pistocchi says,[174] "non multae leges, sed bonae Ecclesiam aedificant."

The right to arrange the plan of administration flows naturally from the right of supervision and is really necessary to make the latter effective. Therefore, with regard to all property which has not

[169] S. C. C., *Dioecesis N.*, 19 febr. 1921—*AAS*, XIII (1921), 228; cf. also Pistocchi, *De Bonis Ecclesiae Temporalibus*, p. 314.

[170] Vermeersch-Creusen, *Epitome*, II, 521; Coronata, *Institutiones Iuris Canonici*, II, 473, nota 5; Vromant, *De Bonis Ecclesiae Temporalibus*, p. 204.

[171] Vromant, *De Bonis Ecclesiae Temporalibus*, p. 204; Pistocchi, *De Bonis Ecclesiae Temporalibus*, p. 314.

[172] "In dubio obsequendum est Superiori."—Cf. Aertnys-Damen, *Theologia Moralis*, I, 54.

[173] Canon 2146.

[174] *De Bonis Ecclesiae Temporalibus*, p. 315.

been removed from his jurisdiction, the local ordinary may give the general norms which are to be followed in the administration of ecclesiastical property. Hence in view of the needs of the parish he may command that the pastor erect a new school rather than a larger church; his knowledge of the conditions in the parish may be the reason why he insists that a church or school should accommodate a definite number of people. While he may determine what improvements or changes may or must be made, the local ordinary cannot validly assume the immediate administration of the work. As has been seen, the law does not give to him the power to administer immediately the property of the parishes.[175]

Moreover, the ordinary may command that church property, and especially parochial property, be incorporated civilly as the possession of the parish taken as a corporate person. If the civil law of the state forbids parish corporations, the bishop may act as the *corporation sole.* However, even in the case of such incorporation the ordinary is obliged to respect the rights of subordinate administrators as given them by the canons. Under no conditions may the local ordinary hold the entire property *in fee simple,* that is with full title to the property in the person of the ordinary.[176] The *parish corporation aggregate* is, if possible, to be in that form which is used in New York State. There the civil law does not permit the members of the congregation to appoint candidates of their own choice as members of the corporation. The bishop, the vicar-general and the pastor are *ex officio* members of the board and they appoint the two additional members. According to the New York Law no act of the trustees is valid unless the consent of the local ordinary or of the one who takes his place in the government of the

175 Although canonical commentators do not give examples of instructions issued by ordinaries, there is no reason to maintain that these instructions must be general in their scope. If a local ordinary has the power to issue a general instruction, it seems that he has the lesser power to give a particular instruction. If he has the power to make a law which binds an individual only, he has the lesser power to issue an instruction to an individual concerning the observance of laws.

176 S. C. C., "De Methodis Possidendi et Administrandi Bona Ecclesiastica in Stat. Americae Foed.," 29 iulii 1911—*Eccl. Review,* XLV (1911), 585-586.

diocese has accompanied the act. Since this law has received the approbation of the Holy See, it should be quoted:

> "The archbishop or bishop and the vicar-general of the diocese to which any incorporated church belongs, the rector of such church and their successors in office shall, by virtue of their offices, be trustees of such church. Two laymen, members of such incorporated society, selected by such officers or a majority of them, shall also be trustees of such incorporated church. . . . No act or proceeding of the trustees of any such incorporated church shall be valid, without the sanction of the archbishop or bishop of the diocese to which such church belongs, or in case of their absence or inability to act, without the sanction of the vicar-general or of the administrator of such diocese." [177]

In connection with this point it is to be noted that in the view of the civil law of New York the people of the parish are the actual incorporators; and, therefore, the people as a whole have the legal title to the property.[178] This differs from the law of the Church which considers that the parish as a non-collegiate person retains the title to the property of the parish.[179] However, the difference in concepts involves no threat to the rights of the church or parish, because the New York law clearly protects the Church. The civil law of New York considers the trustee as an administrator rather than as one who holds legal title to the property.[180] This, coupled with the fact that no act of theirs has any juridical value without the consent of the local ordinary, makes it very difficult for them to bring harm to the property of the church. Finally, the courts of

[177] *Cahill's Consolidated Laws of New York* (Chicago: Callaghan, 1923), pp. 1905-1906.

[178] Bartlett, *The Tenure of Parochial Property in the United States of America*, The Catholic University of America, Canon Law Studies, n. 31 (Washington: The Catholic University of America, 1926), p. 91.

[179] Canons 99 and 1498.

[180] "The vestry or trustees do not sustain to the corporation the relation of a private trustee to a *cestui qui trust*. They are the trustees only in a sense in which the trustees of a civil corporation are such. They are its managing agents and may act for it as fully as the directors or agents of such corporate bodies."—R. C. Cummings and F. B. Gilbert, *Membership and Religious Corporations of New York* (Albany: 1908), p. 277.

New York have shown by their decisions that they construe the law to the benefit of the Church.[181]

Among the commands which the local ordinary may give are those which state that *a collection is to be taken up in the various parishes for some definite charitable purpose,* for example, a collection for the support of the Catholic University of America. Such a decree obliges even the exempt religious in all their churches which are of a parochial nature.[182] The local ordinary may also issue decrees to settle the controversies arising between a pastor and the chapter concerning the administration of a parish the church of which is also the cathedral church.[183] Finally, he may designate which investments are considered safe enough to render secure the money which is entrusted to priests or religious as a pious foundation and which the Code commands administrators to invest safely.[184]

Article 5. The Establishment of the Diocesan Council of Administration

Canon 1520, § 1. Ad hoc munus rite obeundum quilibet Ordinarius in sua civitate episcopali Consilium instituat, quod constet praeside, qui est ipsemet Ordinarius, et duobus vel pluribus viris idoneis, iuris etiam civilis, quantum fieri potest, peritis, ab ipso Ordinario, audito Capitulo, eligendis, nisi iure vel consuetudine peculiari iam alio aequivalenti modo legitime fuerit provisum.

§ 2. Citra apostolicum indultum, ii a munere administratoris excluduntur, qui cum Ordinario loci primo vel secundo consanguinitatis vel affinitatis gradu coniuncti sunt.

§ 3. Loci Ordinarius in administrativis actibus maioris momenti Consilium administrationis audire

[181] Bartlett, *op. cit.*, p. 93.

[182] Coronata, *Institutiones Iuris Canonici,* II, 445; Prümmer, *Manuale Iuris Canonici,* q. 445.

[183] Augustine, *Canonical and Civil Status of Parishes,* p. 198.

[184] Canon 1547.

ne praetermittat; huius tamen sodales votum habent tantum consultivum, nisi iure communi in casibus specialiter expressis vel ex tabulis fundationis eorum consensus exigatur.

§ 4. Sodales huius Consilii iusiurandum de munere bene ac fideliter adimplendo coram Ordinario emittant.

A. *The Purpose of the Council*

Before the Code of canon law there was no general legislation which commanded each ordinary to institute a diocesan council to assist him in his work of administering and supervising ecclesiastical property. Although such a specific board was not required by law, yet the Church had always used the experience and wisdom of a number of individuals that her material possessions might be secure and productive. As has been indicated previously,[185] the economes and the archdeacons had great importance in the temporal administration of the early Church. Moreover, the acts of extraordinary administration, such as alienations, required that the bishop seek the advice or consent of the diocesan clergy.[186] Later the cathedral chapter was authorized to give the consent which the bishop needed before he could alienate church property.[187] In the fifteenth century Pope Paul II issued the decree *"Ambitiosae,"* which forbade the alienation of immovable or valuable movable church property without the consent of the Holy See, as well as of the cathedral chapter.[188] In the nineteenth century the hierarchy of the United States received an indult which allowed bishops, with the

[185] Cf. pp. 21-22, 33-36.

[186] "Sine exceptione decernimus, ne quis episcopus de rebus ecclesiae suae quicquam donare, vel commutare, vel vendere audeat, nisi forte aliquid harum faciat, ut meliora prospiciat, et cum totius cleri tractatu atque consensu id eligat, quod non sit dubium profuturum ecclesiae." C. 52, C. XII, q. 2. Cf. also I Council of Hippo (393), c. 33—Hardouin, I, 879; *Statuta Ecclesiae Antiqua*, c. 32—Hardouin, I, 981; III Council of Toledo (589), c. 3—Mansi, IX, 993.

[187] C. 1, X, *de his, quae fiunt a praelato sine consensu capituli*, III, 10.

[188] C. un., *de rebus ecclesiae non alienandis*, III, 4, in Extravag. com.

advice of their consultors, to alienate property in excess of five thousand dollars.[189]

Therefore, the law of the Code which commands the local ordinary to establish a diocesan council of administration is a normal outcome of the safeguards which the Church has used in the past for the protection of her property. Certainly two or more heads are better than one, especially when ecclesiastical administrators must conform to intricate civil laws in order to safeguard their administrative rights. The ordinary burdened with the spiritual care of a large territory is not expected to be able alone to supervise the administration of the entire diocese without the advice of others. Because temporal welfare is so important for the full exercise of her spiritual obligations, the Church commands *sub gravi* that all local ordinaries establish a council of administration. Apparently the Church's legislation contemplates the establishment of this council on a permanent basis, and not merely as an arrangement whereby the ordinary will have recourse to the advice of two or three competent individuals who are designated on various occasions by a random choice.[190]

The Holy See seems to desire that in mission territories the native clergy be represented on the council of administration.[191] This, no doubt, manifests the wish of the Holy See to train a capable and dependable native clergy, so that the present mission lands may become subject to the common law of the Church as soon as possible.

189 *Acta et Decreta Concilii Plenarii Baltimorensis Tertii,* p. ciii. Cf. also Barrett, *A Comparative Study of the Councils of Baltimore and the Code of Canon Law,* The Catholic University of America, Canon Law Studies, n. 83 (Washington: The Catholic University of America, 1932), p. 80. As the author notes, this indult was granted in response to a petition of the Fathers of the Council; it granted more liberty than the legislation of the Council which declared that sums in excess of five thousand dollars required the permission of the Holy See in addition to the advice of the consultors.

190 A. Couly, "Les Biens Temporels de l'Eglise," *Le Canoniste Contemporain,* XLV (1922), 319.

191 Epist. S. C. de Prop. Fide, 12 apr. 1922, n. 85—*AAS,* XIV (1922), 300.

B. *The Location of the Council*

The Code declares that this board should be established in the episcopal city. If the ordinary is not a bishop, for example, if he has charge of an abbacy or prelacy *nullius*, then the board is to be located in the quasi-episcopal city, that is, wherever the quasi-cathedral church or the curia is located.[192] In mission territory, however, it seems that the council of administration need not be established or convened in the episcopal or quasi-episcopal city, unless the members are close at hand. This solution seems to harmonize with that which the Code in canon 302 makes for the ordinary who wishes to consult the members of his mission council. The canon states that he may consult them *even by letter*.[193] If an ordinary rules two or more dioceses or territories which are of equal rank, or if he holds one diocese *in titulum* and another under his perpetual administration, then he must establish one council in the city where he has his cathedral or curia.[194]

C. *The Members of the Council*

The council must have at least three or more members, one of whom is the ordinary, the *ex officio* president of the council. The vicar-general cannot be a member of the board unless he holds his position by virtue of the fact that he is the ordinary acting as president.[195] The other members of the council must be, so far as is possible, well trained in canon and civil law. Since there is no prohibition against a greater number than two in addition to the ordinary, it would seem that the law would be fulfilled by the appointment of one who is versed in canon law and of two who are skilled in the civil law. Therefore, since priests or clerics well versed in civil law are the exceptions rather than the rule, the ordinary

[192] Pistocchi, *De Bonis Ecclesiae Temporalibus*, p. 320.

[193] Cf. Vromant, *De Bonis Ecclesiae Temporalibus*, pp. 208 and 312.

[194] Pistocchi, *De Bonis Ecclesiae Temporalibus*, p. 320.

[195] A. Couly, "Les Biens Temporels de l'Eglise," *Le Canoniste Contemporain*, XLV (1922), 319; Ayrinhac, *Administrative Legislation in the New Code of Canon Law*, p. 427.

may appoint laymen to the council of administration.[196] Naturally, the civil law which must be known is that of the state in which the diocese is located, as well as the law of the nation. A mere knowledge of civil law in general without any acquaintance with local legislation would not make a person suitable for a position on the board, unless there were none better qualified. It would be worthwhile for a bishop to have a few of his clergy trained in civil law with a view to having them available for his council of administration. The suitability required in addition to legal knowledge signifies that the associate members of the council must have a good reputation and lead a practical Catholic life which furnishes no occasion for reproach.[197] Although in mission territory the same men who are on the general council of administration may also compose the council to be erected for property administration,[198] this can hardly be applied to countries ruled by the common law of the Church, because in the latter case generally there is not the same shortage of priests. Moreover, the very words of canon 1520, § 1, *"audito Capitulo,"* presuppose that the two bodies are to be distinct. Inasmuch as none of the authors treat this specific question, the opinion here maintained must of course abstract from extrinsic authority for any additional proof.

The local ordinary is to appoint the members of the council of administration, but only after consultation with the cathedral chapter. Since canon 1520, § 1, uses the phrase *"audito Capitulo,"* it seems at least probable that if the ordinary does not consult the chapter before he appoints the members of the council nevertheless he acts validly. This opinion is based on the milder interpretation of canon 105, n. 1,[199] which is held by several canonists. These

[196] Coronata, *Institutiones Iuris Canonici,* II, 474; Augustine, *A Commentary on Canon Law,* VI, 581; Blat, *Commentarium,* lib. III, pars II-VI, 530.

[197] Pistocchi, *De Bonis Ecclesiae Temporalibus,* p. 321; Coronata, *Institutiones Iuris Canonici,* II, 474.

[198] S. C. de Prop. Fide, instr. (ad Vic. Ap. Sin.), 18 oct. 1883 ad XIV—*Coll. S. C. P. F.* II, n. 1606. Cf. also Vromant, *De Bonis Ecclesiae Temporalibus,* p. 208.

[199] "Cum ius statuit Superiorem ad agendum indigere consensu vel consilio aliquarum personarum:

"1° Si consensus exigatur, Superior contra earundem votum invalide agit;

commentators maintain that if the superior, who is obliged by law to seek the advice of his consultors or the cathedral chapter, fails to do so his subsequent action is not invalidated by his failure to seek the advice.[200] In territories which do not have a cathedral chapter the board of diocesan consultors has the consultative vote concerning the membership of the council.[201]

The words, "*nisi iure vel consuetudine peculiari iam alio aequivalenti modo legitime fuerit provisum,*" according to the common teaching, refer to the entire paragraph, namely, to the establishment of the council rather than merely to the manner of appointing the members.[202] The ordinary would be free from the obligation of establishing a council only if there already was a board of a different kind established for the same purpose, for example, if the ordinary was obliged by a special law or custom to seek the advice of the various vicars forane in the territory, or if other previously designated persons have been authorized to advise the ordinary in matters of property administration. These exceptions to the law of canon 1520 may originate either in a particular law or in a privilege of the Holy See or in a reasonable custom which has been in duration for forty years. Since the law does not forbid a contrary custom, there is no need that the custom be of a longer duration.[203]

Custom, however, cannot permit the local ordinary to appoint to the council anyone who is related to him in the first or second degree of consanguinity or affinity. Only an apostolic indult can

si consilium tantum, per verba, ex. gr.: *de consilio consultorum,* vel *audito Capitulo, parocho,* etc., satis est ad valide agendum ut Superior illas personas audiat; . . ."

[200] Vermeersch-Creusen, *Epitome,* I, 151-152; Boudinhon, "An nullus semper sit actus Superioris non petito consilio," *Jus Pontificium,* VIII (1928), 29-35; Vromant, *De Bonis Ecclesiae Temporalibus,* pp. 63-64.

[201] Cf. canon 427; Blat, *Commentarium,* lib. III, pars II-VI, 530.

[202] Couly, "Les Biens Temporels de l'Eglise," *Le Canoniste Contemporain,* XLV (1922), 319; Blat, *Commentarium,* lib. III, pars II-VI, 530; Ayrinhac, *Administrative Legislation in the New Code of Canon Law,* p. 426; Vermeersch-Creusen, *Epitome,* II, 521; Pistocchi, *De Bonis Ecclesiae Temporalibus,* p. 322.

[203] Vermeersch-Creusen, *Epitome,* II, 521; Pistocchi, *De Bonis Ecclesiae Temporalibus,* p. 322.

sanction such an appointment.[204] An indult is a quasi-privilege and differs from a strict privilege because of the fact that it is not perpetual.[205] The quasi-privilege demanded by the canon must come from the Holy See, that is, from the pope personally or from the competent congregation. In this case the Sacred Consistorial Congregation has the right to grant such an indult.[206] Couly [207] says that failure to obtain the indult would invalidate the appointment of the specified relatives to a position on the diocesan council. However, this does not seem correct, since canon 1520, § 2, apparently does not verify the conditions required by canon 11, which determines under which conditions laws have an invalidating or incapacitating effect attached to them. Certainly not all laws which prohibit an act or which require a definite form or solemnity are to be considered nullifying if such a prohibited action is placed or if an action is placed without the prescribed form or solemnity. The nullifying or incapacitating effect must be expressly or equivalently stated in the law which thus declares unmistakably the will of the legislator who wishes to add that effect to his prohibition.[208] Canon 1520, § 2, apparently makes the lack of obtaining an apostolic indult for such an appointment a matter of serious neglect, but not one of invalidating effect. Moreover, in canon 1613, which forbids a judge to handle a case that involves a party related to him by consanguinity or affinity within the same degrees, there is no hint of a consequent invalid judicial act if the prohibition is not observed.

The relatives who may not be appointed to the council without an apostolic indult are according to the norm of canon 96, father, grandfather, uncles, nephews, first cousins and brothers-in-law.

Blat [209] remarks that the prohibition applies only to the relatives

[204] Canon 1520, § 2: "Citra apostolicum indultum, ii a munere administratoris excluduntur, qui cum Ordinario loci primo vel secundo consanguinitatis vel affinitatis gradu coniuncti sunt."

[205] Cicognani, *Canon Law*, p. 479.

[206] Canon 248, § 3; Blat, *Commentarium*, lib. III, pars II-VI, 531.

[207] "Les Biens Temporels de l'Eglise,"—*Le Canoniste Contemporain*, XLV (1922), 319.

[208] Michiels, *Normae Generales Iuris Canonici* (Lublin: Universitas Catholica, 1929), I, 275.

[209] *Commentarium*, lib. III, pars II-VI, 531.

of the ordinary who is actually the president of the council and not to relatives of other ordinaries within or without the diocese. Therefore, it does not include the above mentioned relatives of the pope, who is the ordinary of every diocese, nor the relatives of the vicar-general. The opinion seems to be sound, because there will be no undue influence of the president of the council on the other members in view of their relationship to ordinaries who themselves are not members of the council.

D. *The Functions of the Council of Administration.*

The third paragraph of canon 1520 [210] shows the intention of the legislator to remove from the mind of the local ordinary the heavy responsibility which would result if the latter had no dependable consultant. The law also manifests again the great solicitude which the Church has for ecclesiastical property. Therefore, it commands the ordinary in acts of grave moment to seek the advice of the council of administration. Among the acts of grave moment for which the advice of the council is to be sought are all alienations strictly so called, unless the matter is so slight that it can hardly be called an act of grave importance. But even in alienations which in value do not exceed two hundred dollars the ordinary gives the required permission only after he has consulted the council of administration.[211]

Matters of grave moment include any notable expenses which are not regularly necessary for the conservation of the property, but which are indeed quite useful in as much as they will increase the value of the property. Other acts not regularly necessary nevertheless at times are not only useful but imperative for the preservation of the property. Some of these latter acts require the permission of the ordinary, and since they are considered to be of grave importance he must seek the advice of the council before he grants permission. Thus, a subordinate administrator may believe that

[210] "Loci Ordinarius in administrativis actibus maioris momenti Consilium administrationis audire ne praetermittat; huius tamen sodales votum habent tantum consultivum, nisi iure communi in casibus specialiter expressis vel ex tabulis fundationis eorum consensus exigatur."

[211] Canon 1532, § 2.

he ought to start suit in court in behalf of the possessions of the church. Yet, he cannot do so unless he has the permission of the local ordinary, or, if time does not permit this, of the vicar forane.[212]

The erection of a school and the purchase of a parish cemetery would certainly be considered as acts of grave importance and, therefore, would necessitate the advice of the council.[213] The examination of the annual reports, forwarded to the ordinary by subordinate administrators must also be submitted to the council before the ordinary approves, rejects or uses them as a basis for future plans.[214] A donation made to the church cannot according to the norm of canon 1536, § 2, be refused without the permission of the ordinary, and if this donation was of any considerable amount the ordinary would need the advice of his council before he could authorize the refusal of it.

Since the Code uses the words, "ne praetermittat," it seems that there is no invalidating effect intended for the action of the ordinary who fails to consult the council in matters of grave moment,[215] unless the particular action happens to be one for which the law requires the consent of the council.[216] The general law of the Church demands that the local ordinary must have the *consent* of the majority of the members of the council for alienations which in value exceed one thousand *lire* but are less than thirty thousand *lire;*[217] for any exchange of "notes payable to bearer" (*tituli ad latorem*) in return for other property titles which are equally

[212] Cf. canon 1526. Since the power of the vicar forane is really granted for a time of emergency, it will be rare that he will have the opportunity to consult the council of administration. However, in the rare case in which the local ordinary or his delegate cannot be reached for the necessary permission while the council of administration is available, then the vicar forane would be obliged to consult the council.

[213] Vromant, *De Bonis Ecclesiae Temporalibus,* p. 197.

[214] S. C. de Prop. Fide, instr. (ad Vic. Ap. Sin.), 18 oct. 1883, ad XIV—*Coll. S. C. P. F.*, n. 1606; Coronata, *Institutiones Iuris Canonici,* II, 474.

[215] Vermeersch-Creusen, *Epitome,* II, 522; Vromant, *De Bonis Ecclesiae Temporalibus,* p. 208; Pistocchi, *De Bonis Ecclesiae Temporalibus,* p. 326; Wernz-Vidal, *Ius Canonicum,* II, 105, nota 3.

[216] Canon 105, 1°. "Si consensus exigatur, Superior contra earundem votum invalide agit; . . ."

[217] Canon 1532, § 3.

safe;[218] for any lease of church property for a price between one thousand and thirty thousand *lire* if the lease be negotiated for more than nine years, or for any lease which brings a rent of more than thirty thousand *lire* if the lease be negotiated for a period of time which is less than nine years.[219]

The law of foundation is to be understood not only in the strict sense, that is, to signify conditions which have been added in the documents of foundation by the one who endowed the benefice or juridical entity, but also in the broad sense, that is, to signify any statutes made at the time of the juridical constitution of the moral entity in order that the property may be duly preserved or that compensation may be aptly made for any damages to the acquired rights of others because of the juridical constitution of the moral person. Moreover, the broad meaning of the term includes any favorable concessions which were made at the time of the constitution of the benefice or moral person, and which are therefore of greater juridical consequence than if they followed after the act which constituted the moral person as such.[220] Hence, if in either of the above mentioned ways a special law has been attached to the foundation requiring that in specified matters the ordinary shall obtain the consent of the majority of the council, failure to obtain this consent will render any contrary act invalid. Moreover, since the act is null, it has no binding force, and subordinate administrators should not follow the decision of the ordinary, unless they are willing to make themselves personally responsible for any damage which may result from such an unauthorized decision. However, if the law, either general or particular, does not require that the council should give consent in order that the ordinary may act validly, but is fulfilled if he seeks their advice, failure to consult his council will not nullify his subsequent action. The act however will be unlawful, unless the ordinary had sufficient reason to excuse himself from seeking the advice of the council. This opinion also is in line with the milder opinion of those who hold that, when the law obliges the ordinary to seek the advice of his council, failure

[218] Canon 1539, § 2.

[219] Canon 1541, § 2, 2°, 1°.

[220] S. C. C., *Nicosien.*, 9 iunii 1923—*AAS*, XVI (1924), 432.

to do so does not invalidate his subsequent action.[221] However, the subordinate administrator should presume that the ordinary has fulfilled the requirements of law, unless he have moral certainty to the contrary. This rule applies even if there is a possibility of invalidity. Mere possibility does not create a doubt, and even in doubt an action already performed is presumed to have been performed properly.[222]

The members of the council also have the right to have recourse to the Holy See from decisions of the ordinary who has acted without the consent required by law. They have reason to believe that the ordinary cannot otherwise supply the consent.[223] Recourse in such a case would be made to the Sacred Congregation of the Council,[224] and would not suspend the effect of the ordinary's action.[225]

In matters of alienation the council of administration, in so far as it has the right and duty to offer advice in such matters, may and ought to request a new appraisal of the property to be alienated, whenever the members believe that fraud or error has affected the appraisal price. They may also insist that the ordinary adhere to the price which had been agreed upon if the amount of that price exceeded a thousand *lire.* Moreover, if the ordinary should be careless in the supervision of the financial reports which the subordinate administrators have sent to him in compliance with canon 1525, the council should admonish him.[226]

[221] Cf. pp. 113-114.

[222] "In dubio omne factum praesumitur recte factum." Cf. Aertnys-Damen, *Theologia Moralis,* I, 55-56.

[223] S. C. C., *Lauden.,* 14 ian. 1922, ad IV—*AAS,* XIV (1922), 160-161.

[224] Canon 250, § 1. "Congregationi Concilii ea pars negotiorum est commissa . . ." § 2. "Quamobrem ipsius est . . . moderari quae . . . bona ecclesiastica . . . attingunt."

[225] Cf. Ryan, *Principles of Episcopal Jurisdiction,* The Catholic University of America, Canon Law Studies, n. 120 (Washington: The Catholic University of America, 1939), p. 86. The author lists several canons to show that generally recourse from an episcopal decree does not have suspensive effect. He also quotes Van Hove (*De Legibus Ecclesiasticis,* n. 86), who maintains that in a doubt of fact the decree of the superior must be obeyed if the latter probably has not exceeded his competence.

[226] Pistocchi, "Dell'opera del Consiglio Diocesano di Amministrazione,"—*Perfice Munus,* IV (1929), pp. 437-438; *De Bonis Ecclesiae Temporalibus,* p. 327.

E. *The Oath to Be Taken by the Members of the Council of Administration*

In order to prevent any deviation from duty by the members of the council of administration and to impress upon them even more forcefully than does canon 105, § 3,[227] the importance of the work entrusted to them, the Code commands the members to take an oath in the presence of the local ordinary that they will diligently and faithfully perform the duties of their office.[228]

An oath is the invocation of the true God to witness the truth of one's statement. The Code [229] declares that it cannot be taken *"nisi in veritate, in iudicio et in iustitia."* The phrase "in iudicio" points to the fact that some cause of real necessity or great utility alone justifies the use of an oath.[230] Therefore, since the members of the diocesan council are appointed to assist in the administration of matters of grave importance, it is permissible and quite fitting that the legislator should demand an oath from each member as a guarantee that he will fulfill his duty properly. The oath must be taken personally. The use of a procurator renders the act invalid.[231]

The president of the council who is at the same time the ordinary is not required to take a special oath when he establishes the council, because at the time when he took canonical possession of

[227] "Omnes de consensu vel consilio requisiti debent ea qua par est reverentia, fide ac sinceritate sententiam suam aperire."

[228] Canon 1520, § 4: "Sodales huius Consilii iusiurandum de munere bene ac fideliter adimplendo coram Ordinario emittant."

[229] Canon 1316, § 1.

[230] E. Moriarty, *Oaths in Ecclesiastical Courts*, The Catholic University of America, Canon Law Studies, n. 110 (Washington: The Catholic University of America, 1937), p. 2. This author explains the meaning of the phrase, *"in veritate"* in this way: *"truth* demands that the oath-taker testify to the truth, which he knows and as he knows it. In an assertory oath the sworn statements must be in harmony with the truth; in a promissory oath the oath-taker must have a *sincere* intention to fulfill the promise made." He expressed the meaning of the phrase *"in iustitia"* as follows: *"Justice.* (1) In the case of an assertory oath the affirmation or negation which the oath-taker wishes to corroborate must be lawful; (2) in the case of a promissory oath justice requires that the oath-taker be able to assume licitly the obligation of fulfilling his promise."

[231] Canon 1316, § 2.

the territory he took an oath of fidelity to the Holy See.[232] This oath implied his intention to administer church property faithfully in addition to his explicit declaration in the same oath that he would not alienate the property of the *mensa episcopalis*.[233] As is evident from canon 1520, § 4, all other members of the council must take an oath in the presence of the local ordinary. Although the commentators do not treat the matter, it seems that the vicar-general, even if he is president of the council, must take the same oath. This seems to be true because the law does not require that the vicar-general take the same oath which the proper episcopal ordinary must take before taking possession of the territory.

Finally, it should be noted that the local ordinary may delegate another to receive the oath in his name.

Article 6. The Appointment of Administrators by the Local Ordinary

Canon 1521, § 1. Praeter hoc dioecesanum consilium administrationis, Ordinarius loci in administrationem bonorum quae ad aliquam ecclesiam vel locum pium pertinent et ex iure vel tabulis fundationis suum non habent administratorem, assumat viros providos, idoneos et boni testimonii, quibus, elapso trienno, alios sufficiat, nisi locorum circumstantiae aliud suadeant.

§ 2. Quod si laicis partes quaedam in administratione bonorum ecclesiasticorum vel ex legitimo fundationis seu erectionis titulo vel ex Ordinarii loci voluntate competant, nihilominus universa administratio nomine Ecclesiae fiat, ac salvo iure Ordinarii visitandi, exigendi rationes et praescribendi modum administrationis.

In order to fill out the broader outlines of the local ordinary's power of supervision over ecclesiastical property which has not been withdrawn from his jurisdiction the Code states that, in addition

232 Canon 332, § 2; cf. Blat, *Commentarium*, lib. III, pars II-VI, 531.

233 Pontificale Rom., tit. *De consecratione electi in episcopum*.

to the establishment of a diocesan council of administration, the local ordinary shall appoint administrators for those churches or pious institutions which by law or by the documents of foundation do not have an administrator. For, in order that church property may be properly protected, each ecclesiastical moral person ought to have its own administrator who will carry on the work of administration in the name of the Church and not of the State.

By reason of canon 1498 the word *"ecclesia"* includes not only churches in the strict sense of canon 1161,[284] or in the equivalent sense of canon 1191,[285] but also all moral persons within the Church. However, since canon 1521, § 1, also mentions the words *"locum pium,"* it seems that the term *"ecclesia,"* as used in the canon, refers to all moral persons with the exception of non-collegiate moral persons.[286] The term *"locus pius"* refers to non-collegiate moral persons, such as schools, hospitals, seminaries, orphanages, homes for the aged, etc.[287]

Since the canon restricts the appointive right of the ordinary to such cases in which churches or pious institutes do not have an administrator because the common law or the documents of foundation provide for none, it will be helpful to give a list of the authorized administrators who by law or in view of the documents of foundation are accorded the immediate right and duty of administration relative to definitely specified moral ecclesiastical persons.

The administrators designated and authorized by the law of the Code are the following: (1) the rector of a church or of a public oratory relative to the possessions and with respect to the conservation of such a church or oratory; (2) the beneficiary with regard to the property of the benefice; (3) the rector of a non-collegiate moral person, such as an orphanage, a poor house, etc., regarding

[284] "Ecclesiae nomine intelligitur aedes sacra divino cultui dedicata eum potissimum in finem ut omnibus Christifidelibus usui sit ad divinum cultum publice exercendum."

[285] "Oratoria publica eodem iure quo ecclesiae reguntur."

[286] Cf. Pistocchi, *De Bonis Ecclesiae Temporalibus*, p. 330; Blat, *Commentarium*, lib. III, pars II-VI, 532.

[287] Vromant, *De Bonis Ecclesiae Temporalibus*, pp. 36-37, 232; Pistocchi, *De Bonis Ecclesiae Temporalibus*, p. 330.

its goods; (4) the chapter as a whole for the capitular property and that of the cathedral or collegiate church at which it functions.

(1) *The rector of a church or of a public oratory.* That the rector has the right to administer the property of a church or of a public oratory is evident from various canons in the Code.[238]

(2) *The beneficiary.* Canon 1476, § 1, explicitly declares the right and the duty of the beneficiary to administer the goods which belong to his benefice.[239] Since parishes are benefices, the pastor of a parish has the right to administer the property of the parish.[240]

(3) *The rector of a non-collegiate moral person, such as an orphanage, a poor house, etc.* This right of the rector of such an institute is explicitly declared in canon 1489, § 3.[241] Among the various kinds of non-collegiate institutes may be reckoned seminaries. Therefore the rector of the seminary is the administrator of the property of the seminary considered as a non-collegiate moral person. Cox [242] maintains that this is a case wherein the bishop has the right to appoint an administrator other than the rector of the seminary. He disagrees with Vromant,[243] who states that the administrators of seminary property are designated in the law, namely, the deputies mentioned in canon 1359, § 1. However, as Cox well argues, the deputies apparently are not intended to be the

[238] Canon 485. "Rector ecclesiae, sub auctoritate Ordinarii loci . . . debet curare . . . ut . . . bona rite administrentur, sacrae supellectilis atque aedium sacrarum conservationi et decori prospiciatur, . . . "

Canon 1182, § 1. "Firmo praescripto can. 1519-1528, administratio bonorum quae destinata sunt reparandae decorandaeque ecclesiae . . . pertinet . . . ad rectorem, si de alia [*i. e.*, non cathedrali aut non-collegiata] ecclesia [agatur]."

Canon 1191, § 1. "Oratoria publica eodem iure quo ecclesiae reguntur."

[239] "Beneficiarius bona ad suum beneficium pertinentia, ut beneficii curator, administrare debet, ad normam iuris."

[240] Cf. canons 1411, 5°, and 1415, § 3; also canons 1476, § 1, and 1182, § 1; also Bouscaren, *Canon Law Digest*, I, 150.

[241] "Horum institutorum administrare bona sui cuiusque rectoris est secundum normas tabulae fundationis; . . . "

[242] *The Administration of Seminaries*, The Catholic University of America, Canon Law Studies, n. 67 (Washington: The Catholic University of America, 1931), p. 107.

[243] *De Bonis Ecclesiae Temporalibus*, p. 210.

immediate administrators of the property of the seminary, but rather a consultative board in matters of grave importance which touch upon the question of administration.[244] Yet, Cox's conclusion that the immediate administrator of the property has not been provided for by common law seems improbable, since seminaries are according to canon 99 non-collegiate persons.[245] But the immediate administrator of a non-collegiate institute is the rector of that moral person.[246] Therefore, the rector of this moral person, that is, of the seminary, is the administrator designated by common law. However, since a non-collegiate institute, for example, a seminary, may exist in a collegiate institute,[247] the statement that the rector of the seminary is the *de iure* administrator of the non-collegiate person does not mean that he must also be the administrator of the collegiate person. The duty of administering the temporal welfare of the collegiate moral person seems to belong to the econome who is appointed for that work.[248]

(4) *The chapter as a whole for the property which belongs to the chapter and to the cathedral or collegiate church.* Although the common law does not explicitly declare that the chapter is a moral person, yet there is no doubt that it is the administrator of the patrimony which is necessary to enable it to function properly.[249] According to canon 415 the chapter has the right to administer the property of the capitular church and its legacies, even when such church is at the same time a parochial church. *A fortiori* the chap-

[244] Canon 1359, § 4. "Episcopus debet consilium deputatorum in negotiis maioris momenti petere."

[245] Cf. Vermeersch-Creusen, *Epitome,* I, 146.

[246] Canon 1489, § 3.

[247] Vermeersch-Creusen (*Epitome,* II, 499) say: "Nihil autem obstat quin institutum non-collegiale in instituto collegiali exsistat. Sic in Ecclesia catholica exsistunt seminaria; . . . "

[248] Canon 1358.

[249] Couly, "Les Biens Temporals de l'Eglise," *Le Canoniste Contemporain,* XLV (1922), 403-404; cf. Vromant, *De Bonis Ecclesiae Temporalibus,* p. 36. The latter author states that the *"coetus consultorum"* is also to be considered a moral person because it takes the place that ordinarily belongs to the cathedral chapter, as the "senatus episcopi." This view is also maintained by Klekotka (*Diocesan Consultors,* Washington, 1920, pp. 27-36).

ter has this right when the church is not parochial, but merely collegiate.

In other instances the Code does not directly designate the administrators of the possessions of collegiate moral persons, but gives to these juridical persons the power to choose their own administrators, who are then sanctioned as such by the common law.[250] The administrators so chosen are: (1) *The officials designated in accordance with the constitutions of religious institutes and also of societies of men or women who live in community life without vows.* These officials, recognized by the Code as the lawful administrators of the property, are the officials of the institute as such, or of its provinces, or of its houses.[251] (2) *The properly elected officers of lay associations* which have been erected into juridical persons by competent ecclesiastical superiors. These officials are to administer the common property of the association.[252] (3) *The administrators of non-collegiate moral persons if such administrators have been designated by the civil law and confirmed by the Church or by the proper ecclesiastical superiors by reason of concordats, etc.*[253] (4) *The administrators designated by particular law or statute* which has the approval of a competent ecclesiastical superior. Such administrators would be the trustees of a church who according to canon 1183, § 2, may by reason of some privilege or custom be appointed by some one other than the local ordinary. Therefore, even though the administrators are not designated specifically by the common law, nevertheless the law does recognize those who have been legitimately appointed, and the ordinary cannot supplant them with his own candidates.[254]

In addition to the administrators designated or confirmed by the common law, canon 1521, § 1, mentions as legitimate administrators those who have been appointed as such by the donor of a charitable or pious institute. In this event the ordinary cannot without cause

[250] Coronata, *Institutiones Iuris Canonici,* II, 475.

[251] Cf. canon 676, § 2, in connection with canon 532, § 2.

[252] Canons 691; 697, § 1.

[253] De Meester, *Compendium,* tomus III, pars I, 396.

[254] Couly, "Les Biens Temporels de l'Eglise," *Le Canoniste Contemporain,* XLV (1922), 400.

remove the designated administrator in favor of his own selection.[255] However, the local ordinary has the right in virtue of canon 1515, § 3, to supervise the work of the administrators designated by the founder of the institute. Because of this right of supervision he may remove an administrator who has been contumaciously guilty of maladministration, although even then he must follow the provisions of the donor concerning the appointment of substitutes for the management of the property. If no such provisions have been made by the donor, the ordinary's right of supervision would allow him to appoint an administrator according to his own personal discretion. He has the right to remove those whom he himself appointed, even though the term of three years mentioned in canon 1521, § 1, has not expired.[256] Since the reason for this power of removal seems to be the security of ecclesiastical property, he may also remove administrators appointed by the donor of a charitable institute, if it is clear that the administrator is not capable or desirous of protecting the property entrusted to his care.

Therefore, in exact agreement with the former law of the Decretals,[257] the ordinary may appoint an administrator for the property of a church or pious institute only when these non-exempt moral persons have no administrator designated by the documents of foundation, or provided for them by particular or common law. This right of the ordinary is considered to be a duty also, because the commentators say that "assumat" is equivalent to "debet assumere." [258] The ordinary may as a result of this right and duty appoint administrators for associations which have not provided for this in their constitutions, or if they have failed to exercise the right given by their constitutions. If non-collegiate institutes have no provisions for the appointment of successors in the event of the

[255] Canon 1514. "Voluntates fidelium facultates suas in pias causas donantium vel relinquentium, sive per actum inter vivos, sive per actum mortis causa, diligentissime impleantur etiam circa modum administrationis et erogationis bonorum, salvo praescripto can. 1515, § 3."

[256] Coronata, *Institutiones Iuris Canonici,* II, 475.

[257] C. 2, *de religionis domibus, ut episcopo sint subiectae,* III, 11, in Clem.

[258] Augustine, *A Commentary on Canon Law,* VI, 581; Cocchi, *Commentarium,* lib. III, pars VI, n. 289; Coronata, *Institutiones Iuris Canonici,* II, 475.

removal or incapacity of the designated administrator, the ordinary has the right to name the successor. Of course, he also has the power to designate according to the norms of the law the pastors of parishes, the rectors of institutes in which the donor has not designated an administrator, or the directors of diocesan projects which have the status of a moral personality. Moreover, if a collegiate moral person has lost its right of electing an administrator because it deliberately chose an unworthy person for the position,[259] then by reason of canon 178 the right to appoint the administrator belongs to that superior who has the right to confirm the election, or who has the right to appoint the incumbent of the office when the ordinary electors have lost their right. Therefore, the ordinary could in such a case appoint the major superioress of a diocesan institute,[260] unless the religious community had a privilege which stated that this right belonged to some other authority.[261]

Because the efficient administration of church property has so great an importance in the work of the Church and because suspicion must not be permitted to hinder the progress of that work, the law declares certain qualifications which the appointees must possess. These are prudence, suitability for the work and good character. The insistence upon these qualifications is but a reiteration of the high standards set by Clement V (1305-1314).[262] Hence, these administrators must possess a certain discretion and insight together with some knowledge of human nature so that they will

[259] Cf. canon 2391, § 1.

[260] Canon 506, § 4. "In mulierum Congregationibus electioni Antistitae generalis praesideat per se vel per alium Ordinarius loci, in quo electio peragitur; cui, si agatur de Congregationibus iuris dioecesani, peractam electionem confirmare vel rescindere integrum est pro conscientiae officio."

[261] Canon 178. "Si electio intra praescriptum tempus peracta non fuerit, aut collegium iure eligendi privetur in poenam, libera officii provisio ad eum Superiorem devolvitur, a quo confirmanda esset electio *vel cui ius providendi successive competit.*

[262] "Sed eorum gubernatio viris providis, idoneis et boni testimonii committatur, qui sciant, velint et valeant loca ipsa, bona eorum ac iura utiliter regere, et eorum proventus et reditus in personarum usum miserabilium fideliter dispensare, et quos in usuos alios bona praedicta convertere praesumptio verisimilis non exsistat, . . ." C. 2, *de religiosis domibus, ut episcopo sint subiectae,* III, 11, in Clem.

not succumb to the extravagant promises of salesmen, investment houses or their own subjects. Yet their caution must not be so excessive that they fail to appreciate the worthwhile plans and suggestions of others with whom they must deal in the administration of property. They must also have given proof, or at least definite indications, that they have the executive ability to perform administrative duties; and their reputations must be such that the ordinary has moral certitude that they will not yield to avarice, carelessness or extravagance in the management of the property entrusted to their care.[263]

The administrators appointed by the ordinary are to continue in office for three years, and at the expiration of that time the ordinary is commanded to appoint new administrators, unless circumstances persuade him to retain these men for a longer time. The limited term of office for these appointees apparently manifests the intention of the legislator to prevent such offices from becoming quasi-benefices.[264] At times, no doubt, there will be circumstances which will persuade the ordinary not to appoint successors who have all the general requirements, but who at the time may not be able to exert the influence necessary to carry out a project which has already been started; for example, the present administrators may have a greater influence with civil officials whose co-operation is necessary for the completion of the project. Of course, it may happen that there will be a lack of capable successors to the present incumbents; this too will be a reason for not appointing new administrators. If such circumstances are not present to warrant the retention of the same administrators for another term, then the ordinary must appoint new administrators. It may be noted that reappointments are not only permissible, but at times really necessary; for the first concern of the ordinary is the welfare of the church or institute. The sole judge of the presence of an excusing cause in this matter is the local ordinary, who, moreover, is not forbidden to reappoint the same men for more than one additional term

[263] Cf. Blat, *Commentarium,* lib. III, pars II-VI, 532; Pistocchi, *De Bonis Ecclesiae Temporalibus,* p. 330.

[264] Vermeersch-Creusen, *Epitome,* II, 522; Vromant, *De Bonis Ecclesiae Temporalibus,* p. 211.

if the excusing cause continues.[265] The duty to appoint successors to the administrators after a term of three years does not include the obligation to appoint successors to those who perform administrative duties in virtue of a canonical office held by the latter, *e. g.*, to a pastor, or a rector.[266] Hence, the ordinary cannot appoint a pastor or beneficiary and at the same time appoint a temporal administrator to the same parish or benefice, unless he is sure that the pastor or beneficiary is not fitted to carry on the work of temporal administration. In that case the pastor or beneficiary would hardly be suitable according to the norm of canon 459, § 2, unless his spiritual influence was so great as to offset his inability to carry on the work of temporal administration which had to be given to another.[267]

Of course, the ordinary need not wait three years before appointing a successor to the administrator, if it is clear that the present incumbent is incapable or unwilling to administer in a proper manner the property entrusted to his care.

A. *Functions of the Laity in the Administration of Church Property*

Since the law of the Church seeks the security and improvement of ecclesiastical property, it decidedly prefers that clerics should administer its temporal possessions. However, greater financial and legal acumen, or the fulfillment of the terms of a will often furnish reason for the appointment of laymen to help in the administration of ecclesiastical property.[268] In this respect it is to be noted that the laity may only share in the work of ecclesiastical administration; they cannot be designated as the only administrators of any church property, to the exclusion of the ordinary who has the right to visit, to supervise and to review the work of the administrator.[269]

265 Pistocchi, *De Bonis Ecclesiae Temporalibus*, p. 331.

266 Vromant, *De Bonis Ecclesiae Temporalibus*, p. 211; Pistocchi, *op. cit.*, p. 330.

267 Canon 475, § 3, allows the ordinary to appoint a vicar adjutor to a pastor and to define the duties of the vicar.

268 Couly, "Les Biens Temporels de l'Eglise,"—*Le Canoniste Contemporain*, XLV (1922), 401.

269 Blat, *Commentarium*, lib. III, pars II-VI, 533; Coronata, *Institutiones*

Laymen, of course, have no right to administer the property of the church without an appointment recognized by ecclesiastical law. The canon declares that this appointment may be effected in two ways: (1) by the documents of foundation or juridical erection which gives laymen a legitimate title to participate in the administration of ecclesiastical property; (2) by the will of the ordinary.

(1) *By the documents of foundation or juridical erection which give laymen a legitimate title to participate in the administration of ecclesiastical property.* Although the word "*seu*" is often used in an explanatory sense rather than in a disjunctive sense, in canon 1521, § 2, it seems that it is used in a disjunctive sense. Foundation and erection are distinct concepts in law; the former refers to the material element, that is, to the endowment itself, and the latter signifies a juridical constitution of the material endowment into an ecclesiastical moral person.[270] Moreover, it is not necessary that every foundation of an institute be erected into a moral person, since canon 1491, § 2, explicitly mentions institutes which are not constituted as moral persons, after it has pointed, in § 1, to institutes which are erected as moral persons. Yet, each form of institute, that is, without or with moral personality, is a foundation. The law in canon 1521, § 2, admits that a special law naming lay administrators may arise in the act of foundation. This would not be the same as a special law which was made at the erection of a foundation which was constituted thereby a moral person. The pope or his delegate or the local ordinary may add such a law at the time in which the moral person is juridically erected, as appears from a rescript in which the Congregation of the Council has stated that special laws may be placed not only in the act of the material foundation, but also in the act whereby the foundation is erected juridically into a moral person.[271] Hence it seems that the terms "*fundationis*" and "*erectionis*" are not really synonymous, but point

Iuris Canonici (ed. 1939), II, 474; Ayrinhac, *Administrative Legislation in the New Code of Canon Law,* p. 429.

[270] Vromant, *De Bonis Ecclesiae Temporalibus,* p. 29; Blat, *Commentarium,* lib. III, pars II-VI, 533; cf. also S. C. C., *Nicosien.,* 9 iunii 1923—*AAS,* XVI (1924), 432.

[271] S. C. C. *Nicosien.,* 9 iunii 1923—*AAS,* XVI (1924), 432.

to two distinct factors in view of which lay administrators may be appointed.

(2) *By the will of the ordinary.* This refers not so much to his will at the time when the institute was erected into a moral person but to his will at a later time when he desires to appoint laymen to the office of administrator.[272]

In the United States the ordinaries are obliged to observe certain rules before they appoint laymen to assist in the administration of church property. The appointment must be based on necessity concerning which the bishop is the judge.[273] Those chosen must be proposed by the rector of the church because he is better able to know whether his parishioners have made their Easter duty, have contributed satisfactorily to the support of their church, have educated their children in Catholic schools, have avoided membership in forbidden societies and are twenty-one years of age, as the law of the Church for the United States demands. Those chosen must have the written approval of the bishop. The bishop has the right to settle disputes which arise between the pastor and his counsellors. The latter have no right to perform any administrative duties without the consent of the pastor.[274] The consent of the ordinary to a customary practice in this matter is equivalent to a direct appointment.[275] Although no mention of it is made in the canon, the pope as the supreme administrator of all ecclesiastical property, and the Congregation of the Council, which has competence by reason of canon 250, § 2, can also appoint laymen to participate in the administration of church property.

Once they have been appointed to such an office, the laity must perform every administrative act *in the name of the Church.* Hence, they are subject to the authority of the ordinary even though their

[272] Canon 1183, § 2.

[273] *Acta et Decreta Concilii Plenarii Baltimorensis Tertii,* n. 287. This is denied by Barrett who holds that by reason of canon 1521 the local ordinary is no longer free to decide regarding the need of lay trustees. Cf. *A Comparative Study of the Councils of Baltimore and the Code of Canon Law,* p. 198. It is clear from canon 1521 that the bishop is not obliged to appoint lay trustees.

[274] *Acta et Decreta Concilii Plenarii Baltimorensis Tertii,* n. 287.

[275] Pistocchi, *De Bonis Ecclesiae Temporalibus,* p. 332.

appointment is due to a civil law which insists that civil incorporation can be had only if there are lay representatives on the board of trustees. Anything done in the work of property administration without the authority of competent ecclesiastical superiors is invalid, despite the fact that civilly the acts are considered legal and valid.[276] Blat [277] says that administrators act in the name of the Church if they are recognized as procurators of a pious institute which is publicly known to depend upon the law of the Church in its administrative work.

Because they are the agents of the church or institute, they cannot make any investment of church property in their own name; they cannot share personally the profit which such an investment yields. On the other hand, they are not personally responsible for damages which come to the ecclesiastical person in whose name they do business, provided that they have not been guilty of negligence, fraud or any other culpable action, for example, through acts performed without the permission of a competent ecclesiastical superior. In parish corporations the trustees who are laymen may not perform any administrative act without the consent of the pastor or the ordinary.[278] However, it seems that with the proper permissions according to the amount involved, circumstances might urge that they do business in their own names in order that a greater good, for example, the attainment of necessary property at a reasonable price, might come to the Church. This manner of action is, of course, exceptional and must be limited and safeguarded as closely as possible.

Whenever laymen have a share in the temporal administration of church property, they must always render an account of their administration to the local ordinary. This must be done at least once a year according to the prescription of canon 1525, § 1, and, in addition, at any other time in which the ordinary demands it. However, unless there are good reasons for demanding a more fre-

[276] *Acta et Decreta Concilii Plenarii Baltimorensis Tertii,* n. 285.

[277] *Commentarium,* lib. III, pars II-VI, 533.

[278] *Acta et Decreta Concilii Plenarii Baltimorensis Tertii,* n. 287.

quent reckoning the ordinary should not insist upon it.[279] This accounting ought to include a list of the individual property titles, a ledger which contains an accurate reference to the various forms of income and expense as well as the amounts of each and the reasons for the expenses.[280] Investments ought to be explained accurately and with mention of the nature and duration of each investment. Therefore, the account ought to state whether money in the bank is invested, that is, whether it is placed there in order to be productive, or whether it is deposited as a drawing account for the convenient payment of bills. It may be that the money has been transferred into bonds or mortgages at a definite rate of interest, or that it has been used to buy property which can be rented out. All these things as well as any outstanding debts require mention, in order that the ordinary may be able to determine whether there should be any change in the matter or manner of administration.

[279] Pallottini, *Collectio Resolutionum S. C. C.*, XV, tit. "*Redditio rationum,*" n. 63.

[280] S. R. R., 20 feb. 1913—*S. R. Rotae Decisiones,* V (1913), Dec. XV. n. 5.

CONCLUSIONS

1. The Roman Law Sources do not prove conclusively that parochial administration was distinct from episcopal administration of church property. Rather they seem to indicate the contrary.

2. Although the popes had exercised administrative powers over ecclesiastical property of all kinds, this supreme universal administrative right was not clearly asserted in a specific manner before the pronouncement of Clement IV (1265-1268) whose statement received further clarification through Leo X (1513-1522).

3. The Ecclesiastical Sources show that episcopal administrative power was immediate with regard to all church property within the diocese for the first five centuries. Particular legislation thereafter reduced that power until the time of the Decretals of Gregory IX, which declared that episcopal rights over parochial property were restricted to vigilant supervision.

4. The diocesan econome who for five centuries had been the official delegate of the bishop in administering parochial property as well as other diocesan possessions felt the impact of the later legislation which asserted the administrative power of beneficiaries and pastors. According to the law of the Decretals of Gregory IX the econome was to administer beneficial or parochial property only when the benefice or parish had no *de facto* administrator.

5. The pastor had no ordinary and immediate administrative powers before the fifth century. At that time conciliar legislation recognized the need for a division of the temporal administrative power. This was a herald of the universal law of the Decretals of Gregory IX, which stated that the pastor had ordinary and immediate administrative power with regard to the property of his parish. Such power was subject to the supervision of the bishop.

6. At present the pope has the right to administer immediately the property of any ecclesiastical moral person, and for the exercise of this right he needs no special reason. His distributive power, also universal, is conditioned by the natural law, which dictates that the common good furnishes the necessary reason for disposing of the property of subordinate moral persons.

7. In the present law the local ordinary has the right to supervise the administration of all non-exempt ecclesiastical property within his diocese. He cannot rightly be called the supreme administrator of all that property. His ordinary and immediate administrative power extends to diocesan property, to the property of the cathedral church, to the *mensa episcopalis,* to the alms destined for the construction, reconstruction, repair and adornment of *secular* churches at which religious are stationed whether as pastors, or as vicars, who attend to the pastoral cares of the parish in the name of the religious house or community with which the parish has been incorporated, and to the alms which the donor has left for charity in general but without specific designation of the beneficiary.

8. The local ordinary has the right to supervise the administration of property belonging to lay associations, even of the property of those which have not been established as moral ecclesiastical persons.

9. The local ordinary has the power to supervise the execution of wills which leave bequests for some unspecified charitable or religious purposes, unless the trustee of the will is an exempt clerical religious. In the latter case the major superior of the exempt religious has the right to supervise the execution of the will. If the trustee of such a will is a member of a clerical non-exempt religious institute, the local ordinary has the right to supervise the execution of the will, excepting the case where the bequest is for mission work in general and the trustee is a member of a missionary institute.

10. Without an apostolic indult the local ordinary may not transfer the property of one subordinate moral person to another moral person, except in the case of a concomitant division of territory.

11. Funds contributed for the construction, repair or adornment of parochial churches which are owned by exempt religious are administered by the major superior of the religious. Funds contributed for the construction, repair or adornment of churches which are not owned by the clerical exempt religious but are committed to their perpetual use are administered by the major superior of the religious. In this latter case the local ordinary has supervisory rights.

12. The religious pastor of a parochial church not committed to the perpetual care of his community has no ordinary power over funds contributed for the repair or adornment of the church. The local ordinary is the immediate administrator of such funds.

13. The local ordinary is obliged to establish a diocesan council of administration, and when its consent is required for administrative acts failure to obtain such consent will result in the invalidity of those administrative acts.

14. The local ordinary is limited in the appointment of administrators to cases where the general law or particular agreement or privilege have not provided.

BIBLIOGRAPHY

Sources

Acta Apostolicae Sedis (AAS), Romae, 1909—

Acta et Decreta Concilii Plenarii Baltimorensis Tertii, Baltimore: Murphy, 1886.

Acta et Decreta Concilii Provincialis Portlandensis in Oregon Quarti, Portland: Sentinel Printery, 1934.

Acta et Decreta Sacrorum Conciliorum Recentiorum (Collectio Lacensis), 7 vols., Friburgi Brisgoviae, 1870-1890.

Bouscaren, T., *The Canon Law Digest*, 2 vols., Milwaukee: Bruce, 1934-1937. Supplements 1938, 1941.

Bullarum Diplomatum et Privilegiorum Sanctorum Romanorum Pontificum Taurinensis Editio, 25 vols., Augustae Taurinorum, 1857-1872.

Canones et Decreta Concilii Tridentini, ex editione Romana (1834), edidit Joseph Pilella, Naples, 1859.

Codex Iuris Canonici Pii X Pontificis Maximi iussu digestus Benedicti Papae XV auctoritate promulgatus, Romae: Typis Polyglottis Vaticanis, 1917.

Codex Theodosianus, Krueger-Mommsen-Meyer, 3 vols., Berlin, 1905.

Codicis Iuris Canonici Fontes cura Emi. Petri Card. Gasparri editi, 9 vols., Romae: Typis Polyglottis Vaticanis, 1923-1939 (Vols. VII-IX ed. *cura et studio Emi. Justiniani Card. Serédi.*).

Collectanea in Usum Secretariae Sacrae Congregationis Episcoporum et Regularium, ed. *A. Bizzari*, Romae, 1885.

Collectanea Sacrae Congregationis de Propaganda Fide, 2 vols., Romae, 1907.

Corpus Iuris Canonici, ed. Lipsiensis 2., Aemilius Richter-Aemilius Friedberg, 2 vols., Lipsiae, 1879-1881, ed. anastatice repetita, Lipsiae, 1928.

Corpus Iuris Civilis, Krueger-Mommsen-Schoell-Kroll, 5 ed., 3 vols., Berlin: Weidman, 1928.

Councils and Ecclesiastical Documents Relating to Great Britain and Ireland, ed. Haddan, A.-Stubbs, W., 3 vols., Oxford, 1871.

Harduinus, J., *Acta Conciliorum et Epistolae Decretales ac Constitutiones Summorum Pontificum*, 12 vols., Parisiis, 1715.

Jaffe, Philippus, *Regesta Pontificum Romanorum ab condita Ecclesia ad annum post Christum natum MCXCVIII*, 2. ed., 2 vols., Lipsiae, 1881.

Kirch, Conradus, *Enchiridion Fontium Historiae Ecclesiasticae Antiquae*, 4. ed., Friburgi Brisgoviae: Herder, 1923.

Leges Novellae ad Theodosianum Pertinentes, ed. Mommsen-Meyer, Berlin, 1905.

Mansi, Joannes, *Sacrorum Conciliorum Nova et Amplissima Collectio*, 53 vols., Parisiis, 1901-1927.

Migne, J. P., *Patrologiae Cursus Completus, Series Graeca*, 161 vols., Parisiis, 1856-1866.

———, *Patrologiae Cursus Completus, Series Latina,* 221 vols., Parisiis, 1844-1864.

Sacrae Romanae Rotae Decisiones seu Sententiae, Vol. XIX (1927), Romae, Typis Polyglottis Vaticanis, 1936.

AUTHORS

Aertnys, Josephus, et Damen, Cornelius, *Theologia Moralis secundum Doctrinam S. Alfonsi de Ligorio,* 11. ed., 2 vols., Taurinorum Augustae: Marietti, 1928.

Ayrinhac, H. A., *Administrative Legislation in the New Code of Canon Law,* London-New York-Toronto: Longmans, Green & Co., 1930.

———, *General Legislation in the New Code of Canon Law,* London-New York-Toronto: Longmans, Green & Co., 1933.

[Bachofen], Charles Augustine, *A Commentary on the New Code of Canon Law,* 8 vols.; Vol. VI: *Administrative Law,* 2. ed., St. Louis: Herder, 1923.

———, *The Canonical and Civil Status of Catholic Parishes in the United States,* St. Louis: Herder, 1926.

Barbosa, Augustinus, *De Officio et Potestate Episcopi,* Lugduni, 1756.

Barrett, J., *A Comparative Study of the Councils of Baltimore and the Code of Canon Law,* The Catholic University of America, Canon Law Studies, n. 83, Washington: The Catholic University of America, 1932.

Bartlett, Chester, *The Tenure of Parochial Property in the United States,* The Catholic University of America, Canon Law Studies, n. 31, Washington: The Catholic University of America, 1926.

Bastnagel, Clement, *The Appointment of Parochial Adjutants and Assistants,* The Catholic University of America, Canon Law Studies, n. 58, Washington: The Catholic University of America, 1930.

Blat, Albertus, *Commentarium Textus Codicis Iuris Canonici,* 6 vols., Romae, 1921-1927; Liber III, Pars II-VI, *De Rebus,* Romae: Typographia Pontificia in Instituto Pii IX, 1923.

Bouuaert, F.-Simenon, G., *Manuale Iuris Canonici,* 3. ed., 3 vols., Gandae et Leodii, 1930.

Boyd, W. K., *The Ecclesiastical Edicts of the Theodosian Code,* Vol. XXIV, n. 2, of *Studies in History, Economics and Public Law,* ed. by the Faculty of Political Science of Columbia University, New York: The Columbia University Press, 1905.

Cahill's Consolidated Laws of New York, Chicago: Callaghan, 1923.

Cambridge Medieval History, The, 8 vols., New York: Macmillan Co., 1936.

Catholic Encyclopedia, The, 16 vols., New York: Macmillan Co., 1936.

Cavagnis, F., *Institutiones Iuris Publici Ecclesiastici,* 2 vols., Rome, 1888.

Cicognani, Amleto, *Canon Law,* authorized English version, Philadelphia: Dolphin Press, 1934.

Cleary, J., *Canonical Limitations on the Alienation of Church Property,* The Catholic University of America, Canon Law Studies, n. 100, Washington: The Catholic University of America, 1936.

Clergeac, A., *La Curie et les Beneficiers Consistoriaux,* Paris, 1911.

Cocchi, G., *Commentarium in Codicem Iuris Canonici,* 8 vols., Taurini, 1922-1930; Liber III, Pars IV-VI, *De Rebus,* Taurini-Romae, Marietti, 1924.

Coronata, Mattheus Conte a, *Institutiones Iuris Canonici,* 5 vols., Taurini: Marietti, 1928-1936; Vol. II, *De Rebus,* 1931; 2. ed., Taurini: Marietti, 1939. (The first edition is used throughout, except where explicit mention is made of the second edition.)

Coulondre, G., *Des Acquisitions de Biens par les Etablissements de la religion chrétienne in droit romain et dans l'ancien droit François,* Paris, 1886.

Cox, J., *The Administration of Seminaries,* The Catholic University of America, Canon Law Studies, n. 67, Washington: The Catholic University of America, 1931.

Cummings, R.-Gilbert, F., *Membership and Religious Corporations of New York,* Albany, 1908.

De Luca, Cardinalis, *Theatrum Iustitiae et Veritatis,* 5 vols., Venetiis, 1734.

De Meester, Alphonsus, *Iuris Canonici et Iuris Canonico-Civilis Compendium,* nova ed., 3 vols. in 4, Brugis: Desclée, 1921-1928.

Dignan, P., *A History of the Legal Incorporation of Catholic Church Property in the United States* (1784-1932), The Catholic University of America, Studies in Church History, Vol. XIV, Washington: The Catholic University of America, 1933.

Doheny, W. J., *Church Property: Modes of Acquisition,* The Catholic University of America, Canon Law Studies, n. 41, Washington: The Catholic University of America, 1927.

Fagnanus, P., *Commentarium in V Libros Decretalium,* 4 vols., Venetiis, 1696.

Fanfani, L., *De Iure Religiosorum,* 2. ed., Taurini: Marietti, 1925.

Ferreres, J., *Institutiones Canonicae,* 2. ed., 2 vols., Barcinone: Subirana, 1920.

Ferraris, Lucius, *Bibliotheca Canonica, Iuridica, Moralis, Theologica, nec non Ascetica, Polemica, Rubricistica, Historica,* ed. Migne, 8 vols., Parisiis, 1860-1863.

Funk, F. X., *Manual of Church History* (Tr. from 5. ed. by L. Cappadelta), 2 vols., St. Louis: Herder, 1910.

Giraldus, Ubaldus, *Animadversiones ad Barbosam "De officio et potestate parochi,"* Romae, 1774.

Giraud, M. Jean, *Les Registres d'Urbain IV,* 3 tomes, Paris, 1901.

Gosselin, M.-Kelley, M., *The Power of the Pope,* 2 vols., Baltimore, 1853.

Guilfoyle, M., *Custom,* The Catholic University of America, Canon Law Studies, n. 105, Washington: The Catholic University of America, 1937.

Hannan, J., *The Canon Law of Wills,* The Catholic University of America, Canon Law Studies, n. 86, Washington: The Catholic University of America, 1934.

Hermann, J., *Institutiones Theologiae Dogmaticae,* 2 vols., Lugduni et Parisiis: Vitte, 1926.

Klekotka, P., *Diocesan Consultors,* The Catholic University of America, Canon Law Studies, n. 8, Washington: The Catholic University of America, 1920.

Leage, R., *Roman Private Law,* 2. ed., C. H. Ziegler, London, Macmillan, 1930.

Leurenius, P., *Forum Beneficiale* (in tres partes divisum), Coloniae Aggripinae, 1704.

Lunt, William E., *Papal Revenues in the Middle Ages,* 2 vols., New York: 1934.

McManus, James, *The Administration of Temporal Goods in Religious Institutes,* The Catholic University of America, Canon Law Studies, n. 109, Washington: The Catholic University of America, 1937.

Mann, Horace K., *The Lives of the Popes,* 15 vols., St. Louis: Herder, 1925.

Marc, C.-Gestermann, F., *Institutiones Morales Alphonsianae,* 19. ed., 2 vols., Lugduni: Vitte, 1933.

Melo, A., *De Exemptione Regularium,* The Catholic University of America, Canon Law Studies, n. 12, Washington: The Catholic University of America, 1921.

Michiels, Gommarus, *Normae Generales Iuris Canonici,* 2 vols., Lublin: Universitas Catholica, 1929.

Moriarty, E., *Oaths in Ecclesiastical Courts,* The Catholic University of America, Canon Law Studies, n. 110, Washington: The Catholic University of America, 1935.

Nardi, D., *Dei Parrochi opera di Antichità Sacra e disciplina ecclesiastica,* 2 vols., Pesaro, 1829.

Ottaviani, A., *Institutiones Iuris Publici Ecclesiastici,* 2. ed., 2 vols., Romae: Typis Polyglottis Vaticanis, 1935-1936.

Panormitanus, Abbas (Nicolaus de Tudeschis), *Commentaria in Quinque Libros Decretalium,* 5 vols. in 7, Venetiis, 1588.

———, *Quaestiones Subtilissimae,* Venetiis, 1588.

Phillips, G., *Compendium Iuris Ecclesiastici,* ed. Vering, F., 3. ed., Ratisbonae, 1875.

Pistocchi, M., *De Bonis Ecclesiae Temporalibus,* Taurini: Marietti, 1932.

Prümmer, D., *Manuale Iuris Canonici,* 4. et 5. ed., Friburgi Brisgoviae: Herder, 1927.

———, *Manuale Theologiae Moralis secundum Principia S. Thomae Aquinatis,* 4. et 5. ed., 3 vols., Friburgi Brisgoviae: Herder, 1928.

Raus, J., *Institutiones Canonicae iuxta Novum Codicem Iuris,* 2. ed., Lugduni, Parisiis: Vitte, 1931.

Reiffenstuel, Anacletus, *Ius Canonicum Universum,* 5 tomes in 4, Monachii, 1702.

Ryan, G., *Principles of Episcopal Jurisdiction,* The Catholic University of America, Canon Law Studies, n. 120, Washington: The Catholic University of America Press, 1939.

Schmalzgrueber, F., *Ius Ecclesiasticum Universum,* 5 vols. in 12, Romae, 1843-1845.

Thomas Aquinas, St., *Summa Theologica,* Paris, 1885.

Thomassinus, Ludovicus, *Vetus et Nova Ecclesiae Disciplina circa Beneficia et Beneficiarios,* 10 vols., Magontiaci, 1787.

Van Espen, Zegerus, *Scripta Omnia,* 4 vols., Lovanii, 1753.

Vermeersch, A., *Theologiae Moralis Principia, Responsa, Consilia,* 2. ed., 4 vols., Brugis: Beyaert, 1926-1928.

Vermeersch, A.-Creusen, J., *Epitome Iuris Canonici,* 3. ed., 3 vols., Mechliniae et Romae: Dessain, 1927-1928.

Vromant, G., *De Bonis Ecclesiae Temporalibus,* 2. ed., Louvain: Museum Lessianum, 1934.

Wernz, Franciscus, *Ius Decretalium,* 2. ed., 6 vols., Romae, 1906-1913.

Wernz, F.-Vidal, P., *Ius Canonicum ad Codicis Normam exactum,* Vol. II (*De Personis*), 2. ed., Romae: Universitas Gregoriana, 1926.

Periodicals

Acta Ordinis Fratrum Minorum, Quarrachi, 1882—

Angelicum, Romae, 1924—

Archiv für katholisches Kirchenrecht, Innsbruck, 1857-1861; Mainz, 1862—

Le Canoniste Contemporain, Paris, 1881-1926.

Commentarium pro Religiosis, Romae, 1920—

Catholic Historical Review, The, Washington, 1915—

Ecclesiastical Review, The (originally *The American Ecclesiastical Review*), Philadelphia, 1889—

Ius Pontificium, Romae, 1921—

Perfice Munus, Torino, 1926—

Periodica de Re Canonica et Morali utili praesertim Religiosis et Missionariis, Bruges, 1905—

Revue d'histoire et de litterature religieuses, Paris, 1896-1922.

Articles

Boudinhon, A., "An nullus semper sit actus Superioris non petito consilio?", *Jus Pontificium,* VIII (1928), 29-35.

Couly, A., "Les Biens Temporels de l'Eglise," *Le Canoniste Contemporain,* XLV (1922), 305-320, 395-405.

Duchesne, "Les premiers Temps et L'Etat Pontifical," *Revue d'histoire et de litterature religieuses,* I (1896), 238-286.

Gwatkin, H. M., "Constantine and His City," *Cambridge Medieval History,* I, 1-23.

Hirschel, —., "Das Eigenthum am katholischen Kirchengute," *Archiv für katholisches Kirchenrecht,* XXXIV (1875), 259-355.

Larraona, A., "Commentarium Codicis,"—*Commentarium pro Religiosis,* XII (1931), 353-359.

Mayer, H., "Die nicht inkorporierte Klosterpfarrei,"—*Archiv für katholisches Kirchenrecht,* CXII (1932), 478-479.

Nebreda, E., "De loci Ordinariorum iuribus circa pia legata donationesve tum Religiosis tum eorum ecclesiis etiam paroecialibus facta,"—*Commentarium pro Religiosis,* VII (1926), 107-118, 191-198, 261-271, 317-333.

Pistocchi, M., "Dell'opera del Consiglio Diocesano dei Amministrazione," *Perfice Munus,* IV (1929), 437-438.

Suarez, E., "De Pensionibus beneficiis paroecialibus imponendis," *Angelicum,* VI, 217-228.

Turner, C. H., "The Organization of the Church," *The Cambridge Medieval History,* I, 143-182.

Vercauteren, A., "Iterum De Natura Potestatis Vicarii Delegati in Terris Missionum,"—*Jus Pontificium,* XI (1931), 75-78.

Vromant, G., "De donis quae missionariis sive saecularibus sive religiosis quandoque ab extraneis mittuntur," *Periodica,* XVIII (1929), 17*-24*.

———, "De Natura Potestatis Vicarii Delegati in Territorio Missionum," *Jus Pontificium,* X (1930), 19-26.

ALPHABETICAL INDEX

BIOGRAPHICAL NOTE

Joseph John Comyns was born on March 8, 1908, at Brooklyn, New York. After receiving his primary education in Our Lady of Perpetual Help School he attended Brooklyn Preparatory School, from which he was graduated in January, 1925. He then went to Fordham University, where he received the degree of Bachelor of Arts in June, 1929. In September, 1930, he entered the Redemptorist preparatory college at North East, Pennsylvania, and thereupon entered the novitiate of the same Congregation at Ilchester, Maryland, where he was professed on August 2, 1932. Pursuing his seminary studies at Mount Saint Alphonsus, Esopus, New York, he was ordained to the priesthood by His Excellency, Stephen Donahue, on June 23, 1935. After he had completed his final year of theology in 1936, he was sent to the Catholic University of America, where he received the degree of Bachelor of Canon Law in June, 1937, and the degree of Licentiate of Canon Law in June, 1938.

CANON LAW STUDIES

1. Freriks, Rev. Celestine A., C.PP.S., J.C.D., Religious Congregations in Their External Relations, 121 pp., 1916.
2. Galliher, Rev. Daniel M., O.P., J.C.D., Canonical Elections, 117 pp., 1917.
3. Borkowski, Rev. Aurelius L., O.F.M., J.C.D., De Confraternitatibus Ecclesiasticis, 136 pp., 1918.
4. Castillo, Rev. Cayo, J.C.D., Disertacion Historico-Canonica sobre la Potestad del Cabildo en Sede Vacante o Impedida del Vicario Capitular, 99 pp., 1919 (1918).
5. Kubelbeck, Rev. William J., S.T.B., J.C.D., The Sacred Penitentiaria and Its Relation to Faculties of Ordinaries and Priests, 129 pp., 1918.
6. Petrovits, Rev. Joseph, J.C., S.T.D., J.C.D., The New Church Law on Matrimony, X-461 pp., 1919.
7. Hickey, Rev. John J., S.T.B., J.C.D., Irregularities and Simple Impediments in the New Code of Canon Law, 100 pp., 1920.
8. Klekotka, Rev. Peter J., S.T.B., J.C.D., Diocesan Consultors, 179 pp., 1920.
9. Wanenmacher, Rev. Francis, J.C.D., The Evidence in Ecclesiastical Procedure Affecting the Marriage Bond, 1920 (Printed 1935).
10. Golden, Rev. Henry Francis, J.C.D., Parochial Benefices in the New Code, IV-119 pp., 1921 (Printed 1925).
11. Koudelka, Rev. Charles J., J.C.D., Pastors, Their Rights and Duties According to the New Code of Canon Law, 211 pp., 1921.
12. Melo, Rev. Antonius, O.F.M., J.C.D., De Exemptione Regularium, X-188 pp., 1921.
13. Schaaf, Rev. Valentine Theodore, O.F.M., S.T.B., J.C.D., The Cloister, X-180 pp., 1921.
14. Burke, Rev. Thomas Joseph, S.T.D., J.C.D., Competence in Ecclesiastical Tribunals, IV-117 pp., 1922.
15. Leech, Rev. George Leo, J.C.D., A Comparative Study of the Constitution "Apostolicae Sedis" and the "Codex Juris Canonici," 179 pp., 1922.
16. Motry, Rev. Hubert Louis, S.T.D., J.C.D., Diocesan Faculties According to the Code of Canon Law, II-167 pp., 1922.
17. Murphy, Rev. George Lawrence, J.C.D., Delinquencies and Penalties in the Administration and the Reception of the Sacraments, IV-121 pp., 1923.
18. O'Reilly, Rev. John Anthony, S.T.B., J.C.D., Ecclesiastical Sepulture in the New Code of Canon Law, II-129 pp., 1923.
19. Michalicka, Rev. Wenceslas Cyrill, O.S.B., J.C.D., Judicial Procedure in Dismissal of Clerical Exempt Religious, 107 pp., 1923.

20. DARGIN, REV. EDWARD VINCENT, S.T.B., J.C.D., Reserved Cases According to the Code of Canon Law, IV-103 pp., 1924.
21. GODFREY, REV. JOHN A., S.T.B., J.C.D., The Right of Patronage According to the Code of Canon Law, 153 pp., 1924.
22. HAGEDORN, REV. FRANCIS EDWARD, J.C.D., General Legislation on Indulgences, II-154 pp., 1924.
23. KING, REV. JAMES IGNATIUS, J.C.D., The Administration of the Sacraments to Dying Non-Catholics, V-141 pp., 1924.
24. WINSLOW, REV. FRANCIS JOSEPH, O.F.M., J.C.D., Vicars and Prefects Apostolic, IV-149 pp., 1924.
25. CORREA, REV. JOSE SERVELION, S.T.L., J.C.D., La Potestad Legislativa de la Iglesia Catolica, IV-127 pp., 1925.
26. DUGAN, REV. HENRY FRANCIS, A.M., J.C.D., The Judiciary Department of the Diocesan Curia, 87 pp., 1925.
27. KELLER, REV. CHARLES FREDERICK, S.T.B., J.C.D., Mass Stipends, 167 pp., 1925.
28. PASCHANG, REV. JOHN LINUS, J.C.D., The Sacramentals According to the Code of Canon Law, 129 pp., 1925.
29. PIONTEK, REV. CYRILLUS, O.F.M., S.T.B., J.C.D., De Indulto Exclaustrationis necnon Saecularizationis, XIII-289 pp., 1925.
30. KEARNEY, REV. RICHARD JOSEPH, S.T.B., J.C.D., Sponsors at Baptism According to the Code of Canon Law, IV-127 pp., 1925.
31. BARTLETT, REV. CHESTER JOSEPH, A.M., LL.B., J.C.D., The Tenure of Parochial Property in the United States of America, V-108 pp., 1926.
32. KILKER, REV. ADRIAN JEROME, J.C.D., Extreme Unction, V-425 pp., 1926.
33. MCCORMICK, REV. ROBERT EMMETT, J.C.D., Confessors of Religious, VIII-266 pp., 1926.
34. MILLER, REV. NEWTON THOMAS, J.C.D., Founded Masses According to the Code of Canon Law, VII-93 pp., 1926.
35. ROELKER, REV. EDWARD G., S.T.D., J.C.D., Principles of Privilege According to the Code of Canon Law, XI-166 pp., 1926.
36. BAKALARCZYK, REV. RICHARDUS, M.I.C., J.U.D., De Novitiatu, VIII-208 pp., 1927.
37. PIZZUTI, REV. LAWRENCE, O.F.M., J.U.L., De Parochis Religiosis, 1927. (Not Printed.)
38. BLILEY, REV. NICHOLAS MARTIN, O.S.B., J.C.D., Altars According to the Code of Canon Law, XIX-132 pp., 1927.
39. BROWN, MR. BRENDAN FRANCIS, A.B., LL.M., J.U.D., The Canonical Juristic Personality with Special Reference to its Status in the United States of America, V-212 pp., 1927.
40. CAVANAUGH, REV. WILLIAM THOMAS, C.P., J.U.D., The Reservation of the Blessed Sacrament, VIII-101 pp., 1927.
41. DOHENY, REV. WILLIAM J., C.S.C., A.B., J.U.D., Church Property: Modes of Acquisition, X-118 pp., 1927.

42. Feldhaus, Rev. Aloysius H., C.PP.S., J.C.D., Oratories, IX-141 pp., 1927.
43. Kelly, Rev. James Patrick, A.B., J.C.D., The Jurisdiction of the Simple Confessor, X-208 pp., 1927.
44. Neuberger, Rev. Nicholas J., J.C.D., Canon 6 or the Relation of the Codex Juris Canonici to the Preceding Legislation, V-95 pp., 1927.
45. O'Keefe, Rev. Gerald Michael, J.C.D., Matrimonial Dispensations, Powers of Bishops, Priests, and Confessors, VIII-232 pp., 1927.
46. Quigley, Rev. Joseph A. M., A.B., J.C.D., Condemned Societies, 139 pp., 1927.
47. Zaplotnik, Rev. Johannes Leo, J.C.D., De Vicariis Foraneis, X-142 pp., 1927.
48. Duskie, Rev. John Aloysius, A.B., J.C.D., The Canonical Status of the Orientals in the United States, VIII-196 pp., 1928.
49. Hyland, Rev. Francis Edward, J.C.D., Excommunciation, Its Nature, Historical Development and Effects, VIII-181 pp., 1928.
50. Reinmann, Rev. Gerald Joseph, O.M.C., J.C.D., The Third Order Secular of Saint Francis, 201 pp., 1928.
51. Schenk, Rev. Francis J., J.C.D., The Matrimonial Impediments of Mixed Religion and Disparity of Cult, XVI-318 pp., 1929.
52. Coady, Rev. John Joseph, S.T.D., J.U.D., A.M., The Appointment of Pastors, VIII-150 pp., 1929.
53. Kay, Rev. Thomas Henry, J.C.D., Competence in Matrimonial Procedure, VIII-164 pp., 1929.
54. Turner, Rev. Sidney Joseph, C.P., J.U.D., The Vow of Poverty, XLIX-217 pp., 1929.
55. Kearney, Rev. Raymond A., A.B., S.T.D., J.C.D., The Principles of Delegation, VII-149 pp., 1929.
56. Conran, Rev. Edward James, A.B., J.C.D., The Interdict, V-163 pp., 1930.
57. O'Neill, Rev. William H., J.C.D., Papal Rescripts of Favor, VII-218 pp., 1930.
58. Bastnagel, Rev. Clement Vincent, J.U.D., The Appointment of Parochial Adjutants and Assistants, XV-257 pp., 1930.
59. Ferry, Rev. William A., A.B., J.C.D., Stole Fees, V-136 pp., 1930.
60. Costello, Rev. John Michael, A.B., J.C.D., Domicile and Quasi-Domicile, VII-201 pp., 1930.
61. Kremer, Rev. Michael Nicholas, A.B., S.T.B., J.C.D., Church Support in the United States, VI-136 pp., 1930.
62. Angulo, Rev. Luis, C.M., J.C.D., Legislation de la Iglesia sobre la intencion en la application de la Santa Misa, VII-104 pp., 1931.
63. Frey, Rev. Wolfgang Norbert, O.S.B., A.B., J.C.D., The Act of Religious Profession, VIII-174 pp., 1931.
64. Roberts, Rev. James Brendan, A.B., J.C.D., The Banns of Marriage, XIV-140 pp., 1931.
65. Ryder, Rev. Raymond Aloysius, A.B., J.C.D., Simony, IX-151 pp., 1931.

66. CAMPAGNA, REV. ANGELO, PH.D., J.U.D., Il Vicario Generale del Vescovo, VII-205 pp., 1931.
67. COX, REV. JOSEPH GODFREY, A.B., J.C.D., The Administration of Seminaries, VI-124 pp., 1931.
68. GREGORY, REV. DONALD J., J.U.D., The Pauline Privilege, XV-165 pp., 1931.
69. DONOHUE, REV. JOHN F., J.C.D., The Impediment of Crime, VII-110 pp., 1931.
70. DOOLEY, REV. EUGENE A., O.M.I., J.C.D., Church Law on Sacred Relics, IX-143 pp., 1931.
71. ORTH, REV. CLEMENT RAYMOND, O.M.C., J.C.D., The Approbation of Religious Institutes, 171 pp., 1931.
72. PERNICONE, REV. JOSEPH M., A.B., J.C.D., The Ecclesiastical Prohibition of Books, XII-267 pp., 1932.
73. CLINTON, REV. CONNELL, A.B., J.C.D., The Paschal Precept, IX-108 pp., 1932.
74. DONNELLY, REV. FRANCIS B., A.M., S.T.L., J.C.D., The Diocesan Synod, VIII-125 pp., 1932.
75. TORRENTE, REV. CAMILO, C.M.F., J.C.D., Las Processiones Sagradas, V-145 pp., 1932.
76. MURPHY, REV. EDWIN J., C.PP.S., J.C.D., Suspension Ex Informata Conscientia, XI-122 pp., 1932.
77. MACKENZIE, REV. ERIC F., A.M., S.T.L., J.C.D., The Delict of Heresy in its Commission, Penalization, Absolution, VII-124 pp., 1932.
78. LYONS, REV. AVITUS E., S.T.B., J.C.D., The Collegiate Tribunal of First Instance, XI-147 pp., 1932.
79. CONNOLLY, REV. THOMAS A., J.C.D., Appeals, XI-195 pp., 1932.
80. SANGMEISTER, REV. JOSEPH V., A.B., J.C.D., Force and Fear as Precluding Matrimonial Consent, V-211 pp., 1932.
81. JAEGER, REV. LEO A., A.B., J.C.D., The Administration of Vacant and Quasi-Vacant Episcopal Sees in the United States, IX-229 pp., 1932.
82. RIMLINGER, REV. HERBERT T., J.C.D., Error Invalidating Matrimonial Consent, VII-79 pp., 1932.
83. BARRETT, REV. JOHN D. M., S.S., J.C.D., A Comparative Study of the Third Plenary Council of Baltimore and the Code, IX-221 pp., 1932.
84. CARBERRY, REV. JOHN J., PH.D., S.T.D., J.C.D., The Juridical Form of Marriage, X-177 pp., 1934.
85. DOLAN, REV. JOHN L., A.B., J.C.D., The Defensor Vinculi, XII-157 pp., 1934.
86. HANNAN, REV. JEROME D., A.M., S.T.D., LL.B., J.C.D., The Canon Law of Wills, IX-517 pp., 1934.
87. LEMIEUX, REV. DELISE A., A.M., J.C.D., The Sentence in Ecclesiastical Procedure, IX-131 pp., 1934.
88. O'ROURKE, REV. JAMES J., A.B., J.C.D., Parish Registers, VII-109 pp., 1934.

89. TIMLIN, REV. BARTHOLOMEW, O.F.M., A.M., J.C.D., Conditional Matrimonial Consent, X-381 pp., 1934.
90. WAHL, REV. FRANCIS X., A.B., J.C.D., The Matrimonial Impediments of Consanguinity and Affinity, VI-125 pp., 1934.
91. WHITE, REV. ROBERT J., A.B., LL.B., S.T.B., J.C.D., Canonical Ante-Nuptial Promises and the Civil Law, VI-152 pp., 1934.
92. HERRERA, REV. ANTONIO PARRA, O.C.D., J.C.D., Legislacion Ecclesiastica sobra el Ayuno y la Abstinencia, XI-191 pp., 1935.
93. KENNEDY, REV. EDWIN J., J.C.D., The Special Matrimonial Process in Cases of Evident Nullity, X-165 pp., 1935.
94. MANNING, REV. JOHN J., A.B., J.C.D., Presumption of Law in Matrimonial Procedure, XI-111 pp., 1935.
95. MOEDER, REV. JOHN M., J.C.D., The Proper Bishop for Ordination and Dimissorial Letters, VII-135 pp., 1935.
96. O'MARA, REV. WILLIAM A., A.B., J.C.D., Canonical Causes for Matrimonial Dispensations, IX-155 pp., 1935.
97. REILLY, REV. PETER, J.C.D., Residence of Pastors, IX-81 pp., 1935.
98. SMITH, REV. MARINER T., O.P., S.T.Lr., J.C.D., The Penal Law for Religious, VII-169 pp., 1935.
99. WHALEN, REV. DONALD W., A.M., J.C.D., The Value of Testimonial Evidence in Matrimonial Procedure, XIII-297 pp., 1935.
100. CLEARY, REV. JOSEPH F., J.C.D., Canonical Limitations on the Alienation of Church Property, VIII-141 pp., 1936.
101. GLYNN, REV. JOHN C., J.C.D., The Promoter of Justice, XX-337 pp., 1936.
102. BRENNAN, REV. JAMES H., S.S., M.A., S.T.B., J.C.D., The Simple Convalidation of Marriage, VI-135 pp., 1937.
103. BRUNINI, REV. JOSEPH BERNARD, J.C.D., The Clerical Obligations of Canons 139 and 142, X-121 pp., 1937.
104. CONNOR, REV. MAURICE, A.B., J.C.D., The Administrative Removal of Pastors, VIII-159 pp., 1937.
105. GUILFOYLE, REV. MERLIN JOSEPH, J.C.D., Custom, XI-144 pp., 1937.
106. HUGHES, REV. JAMES AUSTIN, A.B., A.M., J.C.D., Witnesses in Criminal Trials of Clerics, IX-140 pp., 1937.
107. JANSEN, REV. RAYMOND J., A.B., S.T.L., J.C.D., Canonical Provisions for Catechetical Instruction, VII-153 pp., 1937.
108. KEALY, REV. JOHN JAMES, A.B., J.C.D., The Introductory Libellus in Church Court Procedure, XI-121 pp., 1937.
109. McMANUS, REV. JAMES EDWARD, C.SS.R., J.C.D., The Administration of Temporal Goods in Religious Institutes, XVI-196 pp., 1937.
110. MORIARTY, REV. EUGENE JAMES, J.C.D., Oaths in Ecclesiastical Courts, X-115 pp., 1937.
111. RAINER, REV. ELIGIUS GEORGE, C.SS.R., J.C.D., Suspension of Clerics, XVII-249 pp., 1937.

112. Reilly, Rev. Thomas F., C.SS.R., J.C.D., Visitation of Religious, VI-195 pp., 1938.
113. Moriarty, Rev. Francis E., C.SS.R., J.C.D., The Extraordinary Absolution from Censures, XV-334 pp., 1938.
114. Connolly, Rev. Nicholas P., J.C.D., The Canonical Erection of Parishes, X-132 pp., 1938.
115. Donovan, Rev. James Joseph, J.C.D., The Pastor's Obligation in Prenuptial Investigation, XII-322 pp., 1938.
116. Harrigan, Rev. Robert J., M.A., S.T.B., J.C.D., The Radical Sanation of Invalid Marriages, VIII-208 pp., 1938.
117. Boffa, Rev. Conrad Humbert, J.C.D., Canonical Provisions for Catholic Schools, VII-211 pp., 1939.
118. Parsons, Rev. Anscar John, O.M.Cap., J.C.D., Canonical Elections, XII-236 pp., 1939.
119. Reilly, Rev. Edward Michael, A.B., J.C.D., The General Norms of Dispensation, XII-156 pp., 1939.
120. Ryan, Rev. Gerald Aloysius, A.B., J.C.D., Principles of Episcopal Jurisdiction, XII-172 pp., 1939.
121. Burton, Rev. Francis James, C.S.C., A.B., J.C.D., A Commentary on Canon 1125, X-222 pp., 1940.
122. Miaskiewicz, Rev. Francis Sigismund, J.C.D., Supplied Jurisdiction According to Canon 209, XII-340 pp., 1940.
123. Rice, Rev. Patrick William, A.B., J.C.D., Proof of Death in Prenuptial Investigation, VIII-156 pp., 1940.
124. Anglin, Rev. Thomas Francis, M.S., J.C.L., The Eucharistic Fast.
125. Coleman, Rev. John Jerome, J.C.L., The Minister of Confirmation.
126. Downs, Rev. John Emmanuel, A.B., J.C.L., The Concept of Clerical Immunity.
127. Esswein, Rev. Anthony Albert, J.C.L., Extrajudicial Penal Powers of Ecclesiastical Superiors.
128. Farrell, Rev. Benjamin Francis, M.A., S.T.L., J.C.L., The Rights and Duties of the Local Ordinary Regarding Congregations of Women Religious of Pontifical Approval.
129. Feeney, Rev. Thomas John, A.B., S.T.L., J.C.L., Restitutio in Integrum.
130. Findlay, Rev. Stephen William, O.S.B., A.B., J.C.L., Canonical Norms Governing the Deposition and Degradation of Clerics.
131. Goodwine, Rev. John, A.B., S.T.L., J.C.L., The Right of the Church to Acquire Property.
132. Heston, Rev. Edward Louis, C.S.C., Ph.D., S.T.D., J.C.L., The Alienation of Church Property in the United States.
133. Hogan, Rev. James John, A.B., S.T.L., J.C.L., Judicial Advocates and Procurators.
134. Kealy, Rev. Thomas M., A.B., Litt.B., J.C.L., Dowry of Women Religious.

135. KEENE, REV. MICHAEL JAMES, O.S.B., J.C.L., Religious Ordinaries and Canon 198.
136. KERIN, REV. CHARLES A., S.S., M.A., S.T.B., J.C.L., The Privation of Christian Burial.
137. LOUIS, REV. WILLIAM FRANCIS, M.A., J.C.L., Diocesan Archives.
138. MCDEVITT, REV. GILBERT JOSEPH, A.B., J.C.L., Legitimacy and Legitimation.
139. MCDONOUGH, REV. THOMAS JOSEPH, A.B., J.C.L., Apostolic Administrators.
140. MEIER, REV. CARL ANTHONY, A.B., J.C.L., Penal Administrative Procedure Against Negligent Pastors.
141. SCHMIDT, REV. JOHN ROGG, A.B., J.C.L., The Principles of Authentic Interpretation in Canon 17 of the Code of Canon Law.
142. SLAFKOSKY, REV. ANDREW LEONARD, A.B., J.C.L., The Canonical Episcopal Visitation of the Diocese.
143. SWOBODA, REV. INNOCENT ROBERT, O.F.M., J.C.L., Ignorance in Relation to the Imputability of Delicts.
144. DUBÉ, REV. ARTHUR JOSEPH, A.B., J.C.L., The General Principles for the Reckoning of Time in Canon Law.
145. MCBRIDE, REV. JAMES T., A.B., J.C.L., Incardination and Excardination of Seculars.
146. KROL, REV. JOHN T., J.C.L., The Defendant in Ecclesiastical Trials.
147. COMYNS, REV. JOSEPH J., J.C.L., Papal and Episcopal Administration of Church Property.

www.ingramcontent.com/pod-product-compliance
Lightning Source LLC
LaVergne TN
LVHW050225080826
844660LV00012B/473

* 9 7 8 0 8 1 3 2 2 3 3 6 0 *